EXPLORAT.

C000145873

This book is dedicated to the memory of Marjorie J. Duckett,
without whose unfailing support this and other books would not have been written.

Richard Duckett

After winning the Cassell's Prize at the Royal Military School of Music, Kneller Hall, Richard went on to study music at the Guildhall School of Music and Drama. He has played extensively as a freelance hornist and has held various teaching posts, including Curriculum Co-ordinator for the City of Birmingham Music Service. Author of the popular 'Team' Brass, Woodwind and Strings tutor books, Richard continues to write and teach music.

Ed Duckett

Ed started playing electric guitar at age 16 and began teaching at school a year later. He graduated from the University of Birmingham with a degree in German and also speaks fluent Spanish. Ed worked as UK and European Sales Manager for several companies in London and the South East before leaving to form Team World Music Ltd. When not at TWM, he continues to play and teach electric guitar. Ed is particularly interested in showing young people how easy it is to make music.

Gary J. Price

After graduating from the University of Birmingham with an MA degree in musicology, Gary joined Birmingham Music Service as a peripatetic music teacher. He has since worked as a secondary music teacher, a primary music co-ordinator, and a curriculum support teacher for a number of schools in the midlands. Gary was formerly Head of Woodwind for Solihull Music Service, and is currently Head of Music at Queensbridge Secondary School in Birmingham.

Paul Slater

After graduating from the London College of Music, Paul toured France with a French Rock group as a keyboard player. He then started as a classroom music teacher but later became a peripatetic keyboard specialist. At present Paul is Head of Percussion and Allied Studies for the City of Birmingham Music Service, while continuing to compose and record.

Cormac Loane

Whilst studying music at the University of London, Cormac Loane was a member of the National Youth Jazz Orchestra of Great Britain. After graduating, he worked as a professional saxophonist before starting his career in education. He has worked extensively as a woodwind teacher in London and the Midlands, was director of Birmingham Schools' Jazz Orchestra for ten years and is currently Head of Professional Development for Birmingham Music Service. Cormac is author of the popular 'Team Woodwind' tutor books and he continues to perform regularly as a jazz musician.

Leo Turner

Leo Turner works for Solihull Music Service as a guitar teacher, ensemble director, curriculum support teacher and teaching coach. He is particularly interested in group teaching. Leo is a teaching mentor for the CT ABRSM course and has contributed to the book 'All Together' by the Associated Board, a publication which focuses on issues relating to group teaching. Leo has also given several in-service training days for various music services, ESTA and the Associated Board. He is also a guitar examiner for the London College of Music. As a performer Leo has given many concerts as part of a guitar duo and has toured Spain, France and Holland.

Ruth Cunningham

Ruth's musical education began in Wakefield where she benefitted enormously from the teaching and ensemble experience provided by the Wakefield Music Service. She went on to graduate from the Birmingham Conservatoire and took a full-time job as a peripatetic woodwind teacher for the Birmingham Music Service in 1999. She plays Flute in various Birmingham orchestras including Queen's Park Sinfonia and Central England Ensemble. In 2004, Ruth qualified as an Advanced Skills Teacher.

Emily Baptiste

After winning the first violin City of Birmingham Symphony Orchestra training scheme prize, Emily graduated from Birmingham Conservatoire with a B. Mus (Hons) degree and went on to gain a PGCE in music. She now enjoys her post as teacher of upper strings with Birmingham Music Service whilst continuing to perform as a freelance violinist.

James Cunningham

James caught the music bug from the brass band tradition in the northern town of Glossop. He graduated from the Birmingham Conservatoire in 2002 where he has since given several lectures in the art of teaching. James began working for Birmingham Music Service as a peripatetic brass teacher in 2000 and currently teaches in a cross-section of schools around the city, including two schools in the King Edward VI Foundation. James conducts many ensembles including the City of Birmingham Brass Band, and has a fulfilling performance schedule.

ACKNOWLEDGMENTS

SERIES AUTHORS	Teachers' Edition: Richard Duckett and Ed Duckett. Students' Editions: Richard Duckett and Gary J. Price
CD TRACKS COMPOSER	Paul Slater Head of Percussion and Allied Studies, City of Birmingham Music Service
TYPESETTING/GRAPHICS	Ed Duckett / Maria Jose Granda Isabel
COVER DESIGN	Phil Duckett
PRODUCTION	Ed Duckett
PROOFREADING	Mary Duckett

Sincere thanks are extended to:-

Cormac Loane	Head of Professional Development, City of Birmingham Music Service
John Clemson	Head of Service, Birmingham Music Service
Timothy Low	Head of Service, Solihull Music Service
Leo Turner	Instrumental Teacher, Solihull Music Service
Tonia Price	Instrumental Teacher, City of Birmingham Music Service
Emily Baptiste	Instrumental Teacher, City of Birmingham Music Service
James Cunningham	Instrumental Teacher, City of Birmingham Music Service
	Instrumental Teacher, City of Birmingham Music Service
Ruth Cunningham	
Joyce Rothschild	Inspector for Music and Drama, Solihull MBC
Trevor Jones	Instrumental Manager, Staffordshire Performing Arts
Louise Jones	Head of Woodwind, Dudley Performing Arts

Robert Vivian	Central Ensembles Co-ordinator, City of Birmingham Music Service
Karen Thornton	Acting Head of Woodwind, City of Birmingham Music Service
Jenny Smith	Strings Editor
Roy Smith	
Deirdre Leeming	Head Teacher, Raddlebarn Primary School, Birmingham
Ted Bunting	University of Central England Instrumental PGCE Tutor www.uce.ac.uk
Derek Andrews	www.futurenet-designs.com
Paul Gardner	
Andi Jepson	DVD Director/Producer at iceni productions - www.iceni.tv
COVER IMAGE	Material created with support from AURA/STScI under NASA contract NAS5-26555
PUBLISHED BY	Team World Music Ltd 2 Reed Mace Drive Bromsgrove Worcestershire B61 0UJ UK +44 (0) 1527 835 878 email@music-tutor.net www.music-tutor.net
COPYRIGHT	© Copyright 2004 by Team World Music Ltd All rights reserved. No part of this book, CD or DVD may be reproduced in any form without written permission from the publisher.
REFERENCE	EXPLORATIONS *Teachers' Edition, Audio CD + DVD* Order Ref: TWM00146
ISBN	1-904776-30-2

Preface

by Cormac Loane

A revolution is underway in the teaching of instrumental music: a new approach is being developed by teachers which unlocks the innate creative imagination of young musicians in a way which reflects the best practice in present-day classroom music, takes account of students' different learning styles and enables them to develop as all-round musicians, as well as highly competent instrumentalists.

This approach is an holistic one where the wide range of skills required by musicians are developed side by side: playing from notation, playing 'by ear' and from memory, playing as a soloist and in an ensemble, improvising, composing, establishing sound instrumental technique and being able to interpret music of different styles and cultures.

EXPLORATIONS introduces activities which can be used by the teacher to integrate the learning of these skills in a way which is relevant to all children, regardless of age, ability, background or special needs.

It is hoped that this Teachers' Edition will serve as a bridge between this educational philosophy and its practical application in the instrumental lesson, in the band or orchestral rehearsal and in the classroom.

EXPLORATIONS, published by Team World Music, actively supports the recommendations of 'A Common Approach, 2002' by the Federation of Music Services, the National Curriculum music guidelines, and joint assessment schemes of major examination boards.

Team World Music offers a range of professional development services which may include practical sessions for teachers, whole-school combined orchestra/classroom one-day workshops, or orchestral and band sessions in schools.

For further information, please contact email@music-tutor.net.

The *EXPLORATIONS* DVD

The *EXPLORATIONS* DVD offers teachers examples of 23 activities being delivered and two example 15-minute lessons. These show how to integrate notational and non-notational activities, including examination preparation, into an holistic framework.

The DVD covers band or orchestral delivery as well as individual and group teaching.

The running time is almost two hours. Where there is no DVD chapter dedicated to a specific activity, this is because the elements of the activity have been presented in a previous, related one. In such cases, the viewer is forwarded to a DVD chapter which contains related elements from other activities so that links can be made. For a full list of activities on the DVD please refer to the Contents/DVD Contents on the pages overleaf.

Before viewing the DVD presentations, it is advisable to read the Preface and the *EXPLORATIONS* Overview. These provide a contextual background to the series and need to be fully assimilated before commencing work with students. Subsequently, each DVD example can be watched in conjunction with the relevant activity page in the Teachers' Edition. These provide further, relevant information about specific activities.

It is recommended that the viewer starts the DVD with the 'Core Activities' section, which includes 'One-Note Rhythm Games' and 'Jazz on 3 Notes'. This is because the four strands of 'Playing By Ear', 'Listen and Copy', 'Listen and Answer' and Improvisation shown in these chapters are the core activities which run through all editions of *EXPLORATIONS*. Thereafter, it may be advisable to watch the two example 15-minute lessons, one of which is individual and the other shared, as these are the most frequent ways that instrumental lessons are organised.

The DVD offers a wide variety of teaching and learning situations. For example, in 'Listen, Copy and Answer (1)', the students have been involved in this type of activity since their first lesson with Cormac, i.e. for 18 months. In 'One-Note Rhythm Games' and 'Jazz on 3 Notes', however, the students are new to the activities and Richard is not their regular teacher. Background information is given at the start of each activity so that the processes and outcomes can be viewed accordingly.

The example lessons by Cormac and Ruth offer a snapshot of a teacher's work at a given moment, implying a past where the activity was started, showing the present where it is being refined or extended, and indicating the future. This demonstrates that *EXPLORATIONS* activities, like all other instrumental work, need to be approached in structured, manageable sections.

Whilst Cormac's and Ruth's holistic style of teaching does not vary from one lesson to the next, the content, pace and ratio of playing to speech might do so.

It is important to stress that none of the DVD activities has been specially rehearsed or scripted for filming.

Cormac Loane
Example 14-minute shared lesson

Staccato Starter, page 12
Listen, Copy and Answer (1), page 18
Examination preparation
Improvising with Ragas, page 43

Ruth Cunningham
Example 17-minute shared lesson

Listen and Copy, page 6
Make Up a Song, page 19
Examination preparation
Memorising (2), page 20
Composing with Copy and Answer, page 26

Contents/DVD Contents

Contents/DVD Contents

CD Contents

Page	Title	Track	Total Bars	Description
4	Pulse Grids	01	[16]	Rhythm accompaniment at ♩=90
		02	[16]	Rhythm accompaniment at ♩=105
		03	[16]	Rhythm accompaniment at ♩=120
5	One-Note Rhythm Games	04	[32]	Eight example 2-bar phrases for copying or answering
		05	[32]	Accompaniment for improvising 2-bar phrases
6	Listen and Copy	06	[32]	Eight example 2-bar phrases for copying
		07	[32]	Accompaniment for improvising and copying 2-bar phrases
7	Listen and Answer	08	[32]	Eight example 2-bar phrases for answering
		07	[32]	Accompaniment for improvising and answering 2-bar phrases
9	Play a Well-Known Tune 'By Ear'	09	[8]	Performance of *Au Clair de la Lune* for listening and pitch discrimination
		10	[8]	First 2 bars of *Au Clair de la Lune* followed by accompaniment for melody to be completed
		11	[8]	Accompaniment for performing *Au Clair de la Lune* 'by ear'
		12	[8]	Performance of *Merrily We Roll Along* for listening and pitch discrimination
		13	[8]	First 2 bars of *Merrily We Roll Along* followed by accompaniment for melody to be completed
		14	[8]	Accompaniment for performing *Merrily We Roll Along* 'by ear'
10	Word-Rhythms	15	[16]	Performance of *Word-Rhythms* for practising clapping, saying-aloud, playing, etc.
		16	[32]	Performance of *Word-Rhythms* for practising playing/using notes in chord
11	Rhythm Grids	17	[32]	Accompaniment for *Rhythm Grids* using notes from the chord boxes
12	Staccato Starter	18	[16]	Accompaniment for *Staccato Starter* using notes from the chord
14	A Rhythm Round	19	[44]	Accompaniment for *A Rhythm Round* using notes from the chord boxes
16	Jazz on 3 Notes	20	[12]	Play-along performance of *Blue Triangle*
		21	[24]	Five example 2- and 4-bar phrases for copying or answering
		22	[60]	Two performances of *Blue Triangle*, followed by two 12-bar blues sequences for improvisation, then a final performance of the theme
18	Listen, Copy and Answer (1)	23	[32]	Eight example 2-bar phrases in $\frac{2}{4}$ for copying and answering
		24	[32]	Accompaniment for improvising and copying 2-bar phrases in $\frac{2}{4}$
		25	[32]	Eight example 2-bar phrases in for copying and answering $\frac{3}{4}$
		26	[32]	Accompaniment for improvising and copying 2-bar phrases in $\frac{3}{4}$
20	Name that Tune	27	[12]	Performance of *Twinkle Star* for listening and pitch discrimination
		28	[12]	First 2 bars of *Twinkle Star* followed by accompaniment for melody to be completed
		29	[12]	Accompaniment for performing *Twinkle Star* 'by ear'
		30	[16]	Performance of *Old Mac* for listening and pitch discrimination
		31	[16]	First 2 bars of *Old Mac* followed by accompaniment for melody to be completed
		32	[16]	Accompaniment for performing *Old Mac* 'by ear'
21	Instant Ensemble	33	[32]	Eight example 2-bar phrases for copying and answering
		34	[32]	Accompaniment for improvising 2-bar phrases
22	Rhythmic Decoration	35	[16]	Play-along performance of *Old MacDonald*
		36	[16]	First 2 bars of *Old MacDonald* followed by accompaniment for decoration with repeated notes
		37	[16]	First 2 bars of *Old MacDonald* followed by accompaniment for decoration with jazz rhythms
		38	[16]	First 2 bars of *Old MacDonald* followed by accompaniment for decorating long notes
		39	[32]	First 4 bars of *Old MacDonald* followed by accompaniment for performing in $\frac{3}{4}$

CD Contents

Page	Title	Track	Total Bars	Description
23	Melodic Decoration	35	[16]	Play-along performance of *Old MacDonald*
		40	[16]	First 2 bars of *Old MacDonald* followed by accompaniment for decoration with <u>raised pitch</u>
		41	[16]	First 2 bars of *Old MacDonald* followed by accompaniment for decoration with <u>lowered pitch</u>
		42	[16]	First 2 bars of *Old MacDonald* followed by accompaniment for decoration with <u>flattened 3rd and 6th</u>
		43	[16]	First 2 bars of *Old MacDonald* followed by accompaniment for <u>rhythmic or melodic decoration</u>
25	Chinese Music	44	[32]	Play-along performance of *Red Dragon*
		45	[32]	Six example 2- and 4-bar phrases for copying or answering
		46	[96]	Accompaniment (in three 32-bar sections accompanied by gong) for performing *Red Dragon*
28	Caribbean Rhythm Round	47	[22]	Play-along performance of *Caribbean Rhythm Round* on percussion
		48	[22]	Play-along performance of *Caribbean Rhythm Round* using notes from the chord boxes
29	Blues Booster	49	[12]	Play-along performance of *Movin' On*
		50	[24]	Four example 2- and 4-bar phrases for copying and answering
		51	[60]	Two performances of *Movin' On*, followed by two 12-bar blues sequences for improvisation, then a final performance of the theme
31	Whole-Tone Improvising	52	[16]	Two 4-bar, whole-tone phrases each followed by a 4-bar slot for improvisation
		53	[16]	Accompaniment for improvising patterns based on the whole-tone scale
		54	[32]	Atmospheric accompaniment for improvising/composing a 'spooky' piece of music
33	Listen, Copy and Answer (2)	55	[32]	Play-along performance of *Echo Mountain* (twice through)
		56	[16]	Play-along performance of *Echo Mountain* with 2nd part included
		57	[16]	Play-along performance of *Echo Mountain* with six slots for improvising answers
37	Salsa Rhythm Round	58	[44]	Play-along performance of *Salsa Rhythm Round* on percussion
		59	[44]	Play-along performance of *Salsa Rhythm Round* using notes from the chord boxes, at ♩=106
		60	[44]	As track 59 at ♩=127
		61	[44]	As track 59 at ♩=142
38	Dorian Jazz	62	[25]	Play-along performance of *Five Spice Jazz* (with repeat after DC)
		63	[25]	As track 62 with example rhythmic variation (for 5 bars only)
		64	[75]	Performance of *Five Spice Jazz*, followed by five 5-bar blues sequences for improvisation, then a final performance of the theme
40	Japanese Music	65	[14]	Play-along performance of *Sakura*
		66	[14]	Three example 2-bar phrases for answering
		67	[28]	Accompaniment for performing *Sakura* and improvising on theme
41	Minimalism	68	[34]	Play-along performance of given ostinati
42	Dodecaphonic Music	69	[48]	Play-along performance of tone-row, ostinato and improvisations
43	Improvising with Ragas	70	[16]	Play-along performance of *Raga*
		71	[16]	Four example 2-bar phrases for copying and answering
44	Jigs and Reels	72	[16]	Play-along performance of *Emerald Isle*
		73	[16]	As track 72 with rhythmic and melodic decoration
		74	[16]	Accompaniment for improvising in folk style
		75	[48]	Performance of *Emerald Isle*, followed by 16-bar sequence for improvisation, then a final performance of *Emerald Isle*

EXPLORATIONS Overview

DVD Reference:

EXPLORATIONS is a series of unique, practical workbooks of musical starting points for creative instrumental teaching and learning. It forms a valuable resource bank of progressive activities to aid the development of general musicianship. It is suitable for both individual and group tuition, for use both in school and at home. It has been designed to complement, rather than replace the traditional tutor-book, and may be introduced at any time from the complete beginner stage[1] onwards[2]. It is not intended, however, to be studied from beginning to end; rather, teachers can select activities to meet the needs of the individual student.

[1] *One-Note Rhythm Games*

[2] *Jigs and Reels*

Each page in *EXPLORATIONS* introduces one or more open-ended musical activities, offering opportunities for a variety of creative work. Central to every activity is the learning or refining of a key musical skill, such as improvising, composing or playing 'by ear'. These are presented progressively throughout.

Through *EXPLORATIONS,* students explore a variety of styles and learn how to create music in non-Western and contemporary idioms. They are given opportunities to improvise and make music using the scales and modes of Indian, Japanese and Folk traditions and can also experiment with more modern sounds from the worlds of Blues, Jazz, Minimalism and Serialism.

The principal aim of *EXPLORATIONS* is to introduce music students of all ages and abilities to musical activities which offer them the opportunity to develop into good, all-round musicians. They are encouraged to articulate internalised sounds, phrases and melodies through their instruments by developing a variety of skills. The development of these skills forms the basis of learning objectives, which are the foundation of the series:

1. To repeat phrases played to them by immediately playing back from memory.

2. To improvise an 'answering' phrase to one that is played to them.

3. To work out 'by ear' how to play phrases from well-known tunes.

4. To improvise with freedom in a wide range of musical structures, styles and traditions, drawing upon internalised resources.

5. To control sounds through the medium of decoding standard notation.

6. To play from memory selected, contrasting phrases and pieces from known repertoire.

7. To play with others, demonstrating ensemble skills.

8. To distinguish between the elements of pulse, rhythm, pitch, tempo, texture and dynamics.

9. To make up some rhythmic and/or melodic variations on well-known tunes, 'by ear'.

10. To compose an ending for an incomplete melody, applying the techniques of imitation, sequence etc.

11. To compose descriptive pieces within the framework of various, scales or modes (e.g. pentatonic) or using a graphic score.

12. To compose a song by developing musical ideas within given structures, and applying instrumental skills.

13. To create a tone-cluster composition with others, demonstrating ensemble skills.

14. To compose through the medium of graphic score by making links between sounds and symbols.

15. To hear sounds in the environment internally, to replicate them on instruments and to use them to illustrate a story.

Listen and Copy

Listen, Copy and Answer (1)

Name That Tune

Improvising with Ragas

Composing with Copy and Answer

Memorising (2)

Caribbean Rhythm Round

Rhythm Grids

Jigs and Reels

Composing with Copy and Answer

Composing Descriptive Music

Make Up a Song

Create-a-Chord

Dot-Dash Phrases

A Sound-Effect Story

Learning objectives 1-4 are the foundation of the core activities on the DVD. These are closely related to the development of speech and language in children, who learn initially by listening and watching and then responding by copying, answering and eventually improvising with words. Awareness of the learning objectives before starting an activity enables teachers to ensure that the child is learning music through the instrument rather than just learning the instrument itself. It is assumed that teachers value these skills and recognise their benefit to young musicians.

DVD Reference:

[3] One-Note Rhythm Games

[4] Cormac's Lesson

[5] Jazz on 3 Notes
(Penultimate Violin Solo)

[6] Improvising with Ragas
[7] Listen and Answer

[8] Improvising with Ragas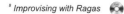

[9] Listen and Copy

[10] Make Up a Song

[11] Cormac's Lesson

[12] Staccato Starter

[13] Jazz on 3 Notes
(String Specialism)

The recommended style of teaching and learning in *EXPLORATIONS* activities is one of child-centred musical self-discovery. It is based upon the premise that all children are inherently musical because, by the time they attend their first lesson, they have already assimilated, through various sources, an abundance of sounds, melodies, structures, styles, harmonies and dissonances which can be effectively tapped by the teacher[3].

It also assumes that children can, with help, discover the diverse musical elements that underpin their internalised reserves of music. This can be achieved by posing well prepared, auto-suggestive questions or 'verbal triggers'[4]. Through this style, students can claim a degree of ownership of their musical skills and knowledge because their natural, creative, musical responses have been drawn out of them by the teacher. The style can accelerate learning and help children to remain in contact with their unique, innate musicianship, whilst at the same time facilitate the acquisition of new musical techniques[5], knowledge and genres. It also helps and encourages students to cultivate the self-motivation, self-reliance and self-confidence which are vital ingredients for the developing musician.

When the activities in *EXPLORATIONS* are presented in the recommended way, as shown in this book and DVD, students will develop all of these skills with ease and confidence.

Teachers, however, can proceed through *EXPLORATIONS* in a manner which complements their preferred teaching style. For example, they can choose to introduce students aurally to the sounds of notes and to their methods of production and then relate them to their notation[6], or vice versa[7]. It is likely, however, that many teachers will adopt an approach which combines these two procedures, thus fusing notational and non-notational studies into a unified whole, which will be pursued throughout a course of lessons. Beginner students may find the decoding of notation an obstacle to learning and performing. *EXPLORATIONS* offers students the possibility of engaging with notation or without, therefore allowing them to participate in their own, preferred way.

In order to support and reinforce this integrated approach, *EXPLORATIONS* provides teachers and students with hundreds of musical prompts and examples as a means of introducing and facilitating relevant activities, including over one hundred and forty cues in standard notation, over fifty in graphic score, nearly forty scales, arpeggios and chords, as well as many rounds, rhythm grids and song/story prompts. Many of the prompts and examples presented in *EXPLORATIONS* are also provided in aural form on the relevant 75-track CD[8], so that students can be encouraged to make the appropriate connections between sounds and symbols.

Using *EXPLORATIONS* to help induce a balance between notational and non-notational activities can assist in the development of an holistic approach to teaching and learning. For example, when students are playing without notation, they are able to learn by listening to, and watching, the teacher[9]. They can assimilate skills such as fingering, posture, phrasing and refining in a natural and focused way, whilst at the same time drawing upon their own reserves and intuition. Added to this, *EXPLORATIONS* provides many possibilities for teachers to work holistically by offering opportunities to perform to students with an accompaniment (on CD), to introduce students to notated prompts, to analyse musical elements such as structure, style, character and mood, to develop expressive qualities[10], to assess, revisit, revise and extend activities, and to allow students to perform informally and formally. By applying an holistic approach to teaching and learning, all the essential components of musical education can be fully and successfully delivered, regardless of the number of students present in the lesson (or rehearsal) and regardless of duration[11].

EXPLORATIONS has been compiled to allow teachers maximum flexibility when planning lessons. The activities may form 'one-off', short musical projects or may be part of a half-term's work on developing a particular skill. Many of the activities, once learned, make effective warm-ups[12]; others can be regularly revised and extended, allowing students to build up confidence and refine a particular musical skill. Suggestions on how activities might be integrated into a series of typical lessons are given on pages 2 and 3.

Individual tuition, which is essential for all developing music students, can be delivered either through individual lessons, or by providing a degree of individual attention to each student in a group lesson, or band[13].

Learning with *EXPLORATIONS* in a group context allows the students and teacher to play together as an ensemble, when appropriate, as well as to perform solos[14]. It can provide opportunities for students to learn from one another and to monitor their progress in relation to others. Self-esteem and confidence can be developed through praise and constructive criticism, and a sense of team-work and loyalty can develop when like-minded students learn and perform together.

EXPLORATIONS group activities present music students (especially the less confident) with a comfortable and unthreatening learning environment because in all activities they are encouraged to choose for themselves which notes they want to (or are able to) play from a given scale, arpeggio or chord[15]. However, suggestions for extending each activity are always provided so that students are expected, for example, to increase their playing range, their technical ability and their capacity to internalise and interpret music.

Whilst, on first inspection, *EXPLORATIONS* for Wind Band/Orchestra and Classroom Band may appear to be in unison, harmony occurs when players of same or different pitched instruments choose notes from chords or scales. Many *EXPLORATIONS* activities, therefore, can only be performed in harmony, and these include 'Word-Rhythms', 'Staccato Starter', 'Create-a-Chord,[16] 'Sound-Scape', 'Caribbean Rhythm Round', 'Salsa Rhythm Round' and 'Minimalism'. Other activities offer a degree of harmonic content through the use of drones and ostinati. These include 'Instant Ensemble', 'Chinese Music', 'Japanese Music' and 'Improvising with Ragas'. The harmonic, ensemble provision in *EXPLORATIONS* for Wind Band/Orchestra and Classroom Band is presented deliberately in this way so that it can be consciously and meaningfully explored 'from the inside' by students, rather than just 'playing through parts'. This approach also allows any group of mixed instrumentalists, large or small, to play together in harmony.

All of the activities in *EXPLORATIONS* allow for a wide degree of differentiation. Teachers are offered scenarios where less advanced students, who may only be able to play two or three notes, can learn and perform alongside quite advanced players. For example, in 'Chinese Music', less advanced players can restrict themselves to improvising with notes from the given drone, whilst the more advanced can use the whole of the pentatonic scale and also add higher or lower notes. This extent of differentiation allows for some lessons to be 'subject-based' rather than the more usual 'ability-range' based. Students of diverse attainment levels can be brought together to work on a musical project, which may be linked to curriculum studies. For example, activities such as 'Caribbean Rhythm Round', 'Japanese Music', 'Jazz on 3 Notes' or 'Instant Ensemble'. This approach, even if used only occasionally, can raise the self-confidence of the less advanced, and may assist them in the development of new techniques by playing alongside, and listening to, more advanced players in an ensemble context[17]. Moreover, all of the related CD accompaniments have been devised especially to allow for the possibility of wide differentiation by presenting simple, uncluttered arrangements. This also means that CD tracks and their related activities can be revisited by students when they have developed more extended technique.

EXPLORATIONS is a totally comprehensive series which can be used with equal success in the practice room, in the classroom and in band or orchestral rehearsals. These strands can be integrated so that students of all abilities and interests can learn and perform together. Instrumental teachers may therefore involve their students in an activity that has been initiated in the classroom, or conversely, classroom students can be included in band/orchestra rehearsals by playing, for example, guitar, recorder or tuned/untuned percussion. If the instrumental teacher is timetabled to teach in school at the same time that instrumentalists are receiving a classroom music lesson, then shared activities can be further enhanced. In this eventuality, some instrumental teachers may feel it appropriate to work alongside the curriculum music teacher in the classroom. Opportunities may be taken to integrate specialist instrumental lessons and classroom music because it can make the learning of a musical instrument more relevant to students. The facility to regularly integrate classroom and instrumental work can lead to a fusion and unity of teaching style between these areas which, in the past, have sometimes been seen as quite separate.

EXPLORATIONS is designed as a sustainable resource suitable for every teacher and student, offering structure and continuity to creative music programmes and therefore comes with a complete teacher support service accessible via www.music-tutor.net.

DVD Reference:

[14] *Jazz on 3 Notes*

[15] *Caribbean Rhythm Round*

[16] *Create-a-Chord*

[17] *Cormac's Lesson*
(Amy models for Ashley)

Teachers' Edition Integration

The *EXPLORATIONS* Teachers' Edition is designed to integrate with any *EXPLORATIONS* Students' Edition or Ensemble Edition. Fold the Teachers' Edition and the teaching notes may be used with any tutorial page.

For example, the teaching notes on page 16 of the Teachers' Edition (Jazz on 3 Notes) will integrate with page 16 of the Students' Edition Trumpet, Flute, Violin (etc.) titles, although the key structure may differ.

Any activity in the Teachers' Edition will integrate with the Wind Band/Orchestra, Classroom Band, Recorder or Classroom Percussion ensemble titles: activities will be on different-numbered pages but will appear in the same keys.

Engagement/Involvement

All *EXPLORATIONS* activities offer students a high degree of individual involvement. At various times they are expected to listen critically to the teacher and to each other, to copy phrases and to improvise, to raise questions and to answer them. However, there are moments when students can be encouraged to remain involved, such as when another student is playing a solo. The following suggestions can be offered:

PULSE
Lightly tap the pulse, either on the body or on the instrument, emphasising the first beat of each bar.

RHYTHM
Lightly tap a rhythmic accompaniment, such as one of those given on the page, or improvise a rhythmic ostinato.

PULSE AND RHYTHM
Lightly tap the pulse with one hand (or foot) and tap an accompanying rhythm with another hand.

DO-IT-YOURSELF DRUM-KIT
Use one foot to tap the pulse and both hands to tap different rhythms. This can be very effective during longer periods of non-playing (e.g. when taking turns to improvise in a 12-bar blues). This is a fairly advanced skill (but great fun!) which can be introduced to students gradually as an independent activity.

CONSTRUCTIVE LISTENING
Listen with focus to other students' improvisations and use these as a basis for further work.

MEASURING PHRASES
Measure the length of other students' improvisations by internally counting, for example, **1**,2,3,4, **2**,2,3,4, **3**,2,3,4 and so on, as when counting rests.

INTERNALISED IMPROVISATION
Mentally improvise a short phrase whilst someone else is playing, perhaps silently fingering at the same time.

Example Planning

Planning for Students within Programme of Study (PoS) 1

This six-week unit of work develops pulse and rhythm control. It offers opportunities for exploring and creating short musical patterns and interpreting elementary notation.

Learning Objectives [for activities in *Explorations*]:

PoS 1: A v Make links between sounds and symbols when using notation

PoS 1: D ii **Repeat** with accuracy short, easy rhythmic and melodic patterns by playing back from memory

PoS 1: D iii **Play** short, easy pieces from notation/symbols, conveying the character of the music

PoS 1: D v Read and play at **sight** short simple phrases at a regular pulse; begin to make links with sound and symbol

PoS 1: E i Play with others demonstrating some basic ensemble skills by listening, watching and keeping time with the group

Lesson 1

- Warm-up: **One-Note Rhythm Games: Activity 2** (p.5)
- Tutor Book work as prescribed by the teacher
- Introduce: **Pulse Grids** (p.4) (Homework: practise the given grids with CD accompaniment and create own pulse grid)

Lesson 2

- Warm-up: review **One-Note Rhythm Games: Activity 2** then 3
- **Pulse Grids** (play a selected pulse grid/combine different pulse grids/review homework
- Tutor Book work as prescribed by the teacher

Lesson 3

- Warm-up: **One-Note Rhythm Games: Activity 3**
- Tutor Book work as prescribed by the teacher
- Introduce: **Rhythm Grids** (p.11)

Lesson 4

- Warm-up: **Staccato Starter** (p.12) and **Pulse Grids** (review a composed or given grid; or combine grids; play as a group or play in harmony)
- Tutor Book work as prescribed by the teacher
- **Rhythm Grids** (combine different rhythms with CD accompaniment)

Lesson 5

- Warm-up: **Staccato Starter and Rhythm Grids** (combine different rhythms with CD accompaniment)
- Introduce: **Word-Rhythms** (p.10)
- Tutor Book work as prescribed by the teacher

Lesson 6

- **One-Note Rhythm Games: Activity 1** then move onto **Pulse Grids** with CD accompaniment
- Tutor Book work as prescribed by the teacher
- Review: **Word-Rhythms** (the students now compose their own word-rhythms)

Planning for Students within Programme of Study (PoS) 2

This six-week unit of work develops skills for improvising in a jazz idiom. Students learn a 12-bar blues piece and create improvised solos in a performance context.

Learning Objectives [for activities in *Explorations*]:

PoS 2: A iv Recognise and convey simple structures in playing, e.g. repetition of rhythmic and melodic phrases

PoS 2: C i Improvise rhythmic and melodic phrases freely or within given structures, individually or as a group

PoS 2: C ii Compose by developing musical ideas within given simple structures and applying instrumental skills

PoS 2: D i Work out **by ear** how to play easy, well-known tunes in simple keys

PoS 2: E ii Explore, discuss and convey the character of the music

Lesson 1

- Warm-up: **One-Note Rhythm Games: Activity 2&3** (p.5)
- **Listen and Answer** (p.7)
- Scales (as prescribed) and repertoire work (solo/group)

Lesson 2

- Warm-up: **Listen and Answer**
- **Composing with Copy and Answer** (p.26)
- Scales (as prescribed) and repertoire work (solo/group)

Lesson 3

- Warm-up: **Composing with Copy and Answer**
- Scales (as prescribed) and repertoire work (solo/group)
- **Name that Tune** (p.20) (Homework: notate one of the **'Play by Ear'** prompts with the aid of the CD)

Lesson 4

- Warm-up: **Listen and Answer/Name that Tune** (p.20)
- Scales (as prescribed) and repertoire work (solo/group)
- **Jazz on 3 Notes** (p.16). Learn *'Blue Triangle'* with an improvised accompaniment or with the aid of the CD (homework: practise *'Blue Triangle'* with the CD accompaniment)

Lesson 5

- Warm-up: **Create-a-Chord** (p.12)
  Scales (as prescribed) and repertoire work (solo/group)
- **Jazz on 3 Notes:** Review *'Blue Triangle'*, then practise
- improvising phrases as directed with the CD accompaniment (homework: practise improvising phrases with the aid of the CD)

Lesson 6

- Warm-up: **Create-a-Chord**
- Scales (as prescribed) and repertoire work (solo/group)
- **Jazz on 3 Notes:** Review *'Blue Triangle'*, then practise improvising phrases as directed
- Perform *'Blue Triangle'* with CD accompaniment

Example Planning

Planning for Students within Programme of Study (PoS) 3

This six-week unit of work introduces students to the sound-world of the whole-tone scale. They apply their knowledge and understanding to create a descriptive piece of music.

Learning Objectives [for activities in *Explorations*]:

PoS 3: A i   Listen with concentration, responding to the expressive character of the music, using their experiences to form their playing

PoS 3: C i   Improvise in a variety of genres and styles, sustaining and developing ideas and achieving different intended musical effects with instrument

PoS 3: C ii Apply knowledge and understanding of the instrument to compose with an understanding of musical idiom

PoS 3: D iii **Repeat** with accuracy moderately short musical phrases (melodic and rhythmic) from memory

Lesson 1

- Warm-up: **Create-a-Chord** (p.12)
- Introduce: **Whole-Tone Improvising** (p.31) (homework: learn whole-tone scale from memory)
- Tutor Book work, scale and/or repertoire study, as appropriate

Lesson 2

- Warm-up: **Create-a-Chord**
- **Whole-Tone Improvising:** Review whole-tone scale and move on to example improvisation rhythms (homework: practise improvising different rhythms with the aid of the CD)
- Tutor Book work, scale and/or repertoire study, as appropriate

Lesson 3

- Warm-up: **Dot-Dash Phrases** (p.13) (use the whole-tone scale)
- **Whole-Tone Improvising:** Review whole-tone scale and create new improvised rhythms. Perform with the given piano ostinato
- Tutor Book work, scale and/or repertoire study, as appropriate

Lesson 4

- Warm-up: **Dot-Dash Phrases** (use the whole-tone scale)
- Introduce **Composing Descriptive Music** (p.39), focusing on the example title *'Seascape'* (homework: create own seascape composition using the whole-tone scale
- Tutor Book work, scale and/or repertoire study, as appropriate

Lesson 5

- Warm-up: **Listen and Copy** (p.6) (use notes from the whole-tone scale)
- Review homework: *'Seascape'* composition. Appraise and
- refine as appropriate
  Tutor Book work, scale and/or repertoire study, as appropriate

Lesson 6

- Warm-up: **Listen and Copy** (use notes from the whole-tone scale)
- Perform *'Seascape'* to an audience
- Tutor book work, scale and/or repertoire study, as appropriate

Planning for Students within Programme of Study (PoS) 4

This six-week unit of work on Japanese music runs alongside preparation for grade V practical examination. During the unit the student learns how to perform, improvise and compose using a traditional Japanese scale.

Learning Objectives [for activities in *Explorations*]:

PoS 4: A i   Use their listening skills and experiences of a variety of musical styles and traditions to inform interpretations

PoS 4: C i   Improvise with freedom in a wide range of musical genres, styles and traditions, drawing on internalised sounds

PoS 4: C iii Apply their knowledge of style, characteristics and historical/social background in order to interpret music with understanding and insight; evaluate how interpretation reflects the context in which the music was created and is performed and heard

PoS 4: D ii **Repeat** with accuracy phrases of a moderate length and complexity in a variety of styles

Lesson 1

- Warm-up: Review *'Red Dragon'* in **Chinese Music** (p.25)
- Review and rework the improvisation activity in **Chinese Music**
- Exam preparation for grade V

Lesson 2

- Warm-up: **Listen, Copy and Answer** (p.18)
- Introduce: **Japanese Music** (p.40) Learn the 'In' scale from memory
- Learn and perform *'Sakura'*
- Exam preparation for grade V

Lesson 3

- Warm-up: Review **Composing with Copy and Answer** (p.26)
- Exam preparation for grade V
- **Japanese Music.** Review *'Sakura'* and begin work on 2- and 4-bar improvisations. (Homework: practise improvising phrases using the 'In' scale)

Lesson 4

- Warm-up: **Rhythm Grids** (p.11)
- Exam preparation for grade V
- **Japanese Music.** Perform *'Sakura'* with improvised passages with the CD accompaniment

Lesson 5

- Warm-up: **Listen, Copy and Answer** (p.33). Review with CD accompaniment
- Exam preparation for grade V
- **Japanese Music.** Use the 'In' scale to begin to compose your own Japanese style melody. (Homework: finish composing Japanese style melody)

Lesson 6

- Warm-up: **Rhythm Grids** (p.11)
- **Japanese Music.** Perform own Japanese style melody based on the 'In' scale
- Exam preparation for grade V

Pulse Grids

- These pulse grids, for one or more players, can be clapped, sung, or played on any note(s).
- Starting with the first grid, play each row from left to right, maintaining a 4-beat pulse throughout. *[CD01, CD02, CD03]*
- Then play the grid in different ways, for example, in unison, in harmony, and in rounds.

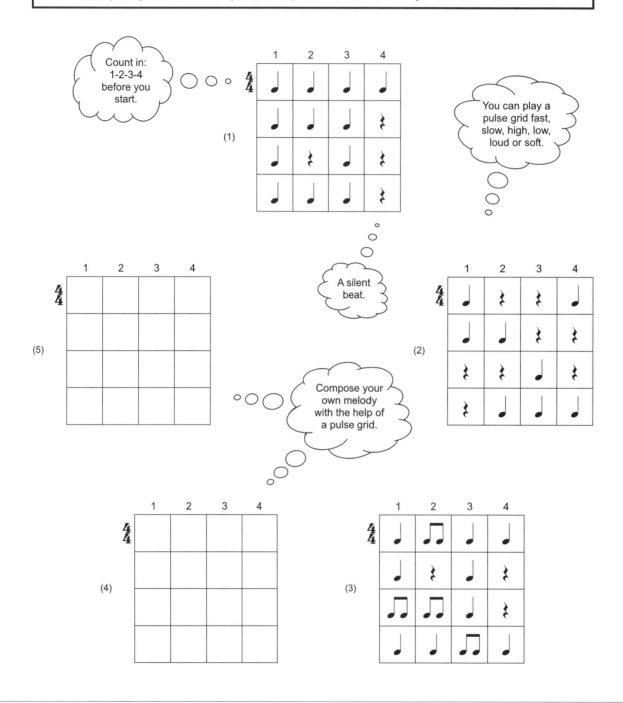

EXPLORATIONS Recorder Students' Edition

POINTS TO NOTE ON THE DVD

PULSE GRIDS:

Please refer to examples of pulse and rhythm work in DVD chapter **RHYTHM GRIDS**.

LEARNING OBJECTIVES

To recognise and discriminate between the musical elements of pulse, rhythm, pitch, tempo and dynamics.

These Pulse Grid activities can be introduced through clapping, speaking rhythms and singing, using different tempi and dynamics.

To begin, it can be helpful to assign 'word-rhythms' or French rhythm terms to respective note values. For example:

(Grid 3)

I'd like to have my lunch now

Alternatively, students may invent their own word-rhythms. Before attempting to play them, students can clap a 4-beat pulse whilst the teacher plays the rhythm (and vice versa).

The CD accompaniments on tracks 01, 02 and 03 are all 16 bars long, thus allowing any grid to be performed four times in various ways. The tempo of the three tracks are ♩=90, ♩=105 and ♩=120 respectively.

HOMEWORK ACTIVITIES:

(1) Practise the given grids in a variety of different ways with the relevant CD tracks.

(2) Compose a melody using a blank grid.

BACKGROUND INFORMATION

This Pulse Grid activity builds upon the skills developed in 'One-Note Rhythm Games' and 'Word-Rhythms'.

The activity is intended to help students to read staff notation by separating the elements of pulse, rhythm, rests, tempo and dynamics.

The pulse grids can also be used as a compositional device and as a means of learning about and exploring harmony, unison and rounds.

TEACHING IN GROUPS

One student can be asked to clap, or play, any one or two lines of a chosen pulse grid and the other players asked to identify it.

Half of the group can play the notes on their instruments whilst the other half claps the rests. All three grids can be played simultaneously (and repeated) on different notes to produce harmony. For example Grid 1 on C, Grid 2 on E and Grid 3 on G.

In order to establish the concept of 'group pulse', students can be asked to play the first two bars of a grid together (perhaps in harmony) and then 'think silently' through the next two, and so on, alternately, to the end of a grid.

DIFFERENTIATION

When interpreting the rhythms for the first time, students may choose to play them on any note(s) that they are able to produce easily. More advanced players may interpret the rhythms using notes from a scale or arpeggio, for example.

EXTENSION ACTIVITIES

When using the grids for composing, they may also be played diagonally or vertically and include a combination of rhythms from two or more grids. Students can create their own melodies by adding notes to the blank boxes. They could write letter-names over the notes in order to make a record of their composition.

➡ 'Rhythm Grids'; 'Caribbean Rhythm Round'.

One-Note Rhythm Games

- These one-note activities, for one or more players, are example prompts for extended rhythm work and general musicianship.

- In Activity 1, one player thinks of a popular tune and plays its rhythm on one note. The other player(s) must then name it and play it.

- In Activity 2, one player plays a 2-bar phrase on one note, and the other(s) immediately copy. *[CD04, CD05]*

- In Activity 3, one player plays a 2-bar phrase on one note and another player immediately plays a 2-bar answering phrase. *[CD04, CD05]*

- A 4-beat pulse should be maintained through Activities 2 and 3.

ACTIVITY 1

(Answer: 'Jingle Bells')

(etc)

ACTIVITY 2

1st PLAYER   *OTHER PLAYER(S)*

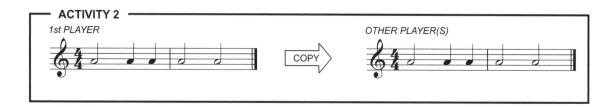

COPY

ACTIVITY 3

1st PLAYER   *OTHER PLAYER(S)*

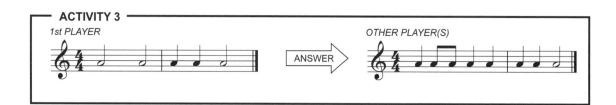

ANSWER

KEYBOARD ACCOMPANIMENT (ACTIVITIES 2&3)

Brisk blues tempo

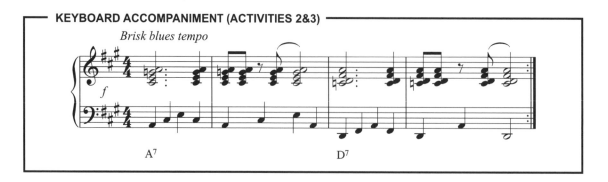

A^7 D^7

EXPLORATIONS Recorder Students' Edition

POINTS TO NOTE ON THE DVD

ONE-NOTE RHYTHM GAMES

- ACTIVITY 1: In this large group setting, one teacher leads activities with their instrument while another accompanies.

- ACTIVITY 2: Dynamics are introduced and the musical term defined. The opportunity for a student to lead the band is voluntary, not obligatory. Notice how Joseph performs sensitively with the accompaniment.

- ACTIVITY 3: Every student is a soloist and, momentarily, the leader of the group. This is a great confidence-builder.

LEARNING OBJECTIVES

To repeat with accuracy short, easy patterns by playing back from memory; to improvise an 'answering' phrase to a rhythmic pattern played by the teacher (or heard on CD).

These one-note games can be introduced through clapping, speaking rhythms, or singing. Singing can help students to form a clear aural perception of what is to be played.

To begin with, it can be helpful to assign 'word-rhythms' to respective note values. For example:

This technique can often be a useful reference point for some students when starting to improvise. Using 'word-rhythms' can be equally beneficial when learning to decode notation.

When introducing Activity 3 for the first time, students should be given the choice either to copy the 2-bar phrase played to them, or to answer it when they feel confident to do so.

Confidence can be developed by making improvisation a normal and regular part of the learning process, both in lessons and in practice.

HOMEWORK ACTIVITIES:

(1) Copy or 'answer' the given phrases using CD track 04.

(2) Improvise 2- and 4-bar phrases using CD track 05.

BACKGROUND INFORMATION

ACTIVITY 1

This encourages students to hear a melody in their heads (internalising), and to play the rhythm of the melody on one note of their instrument.

ACTIVITIES 2 and 3

These are sometimes known as 'call-and-echo' and 'call-and-response', and are two basic techniques of learning music in many cultures around the world.

Copying and 'answering' phrases are valuable musical skills for students of all standards, and can be undertaken individually or in any size of group.

TEACHING IN GROUPS

ACTIVITY 1

After each student has played the rhythm of their chosen melody and it has been identified, the whole group can then play the rhythm. The teacher may join in with the melody, if appropriate.

ACTIVITIES 2 and 3

In the first instance, the group can copy or 'answer' 2-bar phrases played by the teacher. At a later stage, students can take turns to improvise a 2-bar prompt, which can then be copied or 'answered' by the other player(s). This ensures that all students are engaged in the activities for the maximum amount of time.

When a sufficient level of confidence has been reached, students can be encouraged to stand up just prior to performing their solo. This is an effective way of replicating a performance situation within a lesson context.

DIFFERENTIATION

All three activities can be performed by players of any technical ability, from complete beginner to advanced. If the student is unable to play the given note, the teacher can suggest a different one.

EXTENSION ACTIVITIES

More complex rhythms can gradually be introduced, including quavers in compound time.

Activities 2 and 3 could be performed using 'swing' quavers instead of the given 'straight' quavers.

➡ 'Listen and Copy'; 'Listen and Answer'.

Listen and Copy

EXPLORATIONS

- This listen and copy activity is for one or more players.

- Play each of the 2-bar phrases below. Each phrase should then be copied by one or more players. *[CD06, CD07]*

- A 4-beat pulse should be maintained throughout.

EXAMPLE 2-BAR PHRASE

PHRASE ONE — 1st PLAYER

COPY OF PHRASE ONE — OTHER PLAYER(S)

COPY

1st PLAYER

OTHER PLAYER(S)

(1) COPY

(2) COPY

To begin with, it can be helpful to watch the finger movements of the 1st player, as well as listening.

(3) COPY

(4) COPY

(5) COPY

(6) COPY

(7) COPY

Now make up your own 2-bar phrases for other players to copy.

(8) COPY

EXPLORATIONS Recorder Students' Edition

POINTS TO NOTE ON THE DVD

LISTEN AND COPY

- The teacher uses a scale set for a relevant examination - D major. This helps to place the scale into a relevant playing context and prepares the student for an examination piece in D.

- The teacher refers to technique by distinguishing between slurring and tonguing in an aural context.

- She asks the student to correct his mistake rather than to explain to him what the problem is. This places the responsibility for focused listening onto the student.

LEARNING OBJECTIVES

To repeat with accuracy short, easy patterns by playing back from memory.

This 'Listen and Copy' activity can be introduced through clapping and singing. Singing a phrase before trying to play it helps students to internalize.

It can be helpful to assign 'word-rhythms' or French rhythm terms to note values. For example:

In the first instance, students may find it easier to copy phrases comprising mainly repeated notes in step-wise form, as in examples 1 to 4. In the first lesson these phrases can be played on just one or two notes, expanding to three or four in subsequent lessons. The activity can then be used as an effective, regular warm-up.

After the activity has been performed, students can be introduced to reading the notes from staff notation.

HOMEWORK ACTIVITIES:

(1) Copy the given 2-bar phrases using CD track 06.

(2) Hum or sing a 2-bar phrase and then copy it on the instrument (or vice-versa) using CD track 07.

BACKGROUND INFORMATION

This activity, which is sometimes known as 'call-and-echo', builds upon the skills developed in ACTIVITY 2 of 'One-Note Rhythm Games'.

Using 'Listen and Copy' offers students the opportunity to learn to play their first notes by listening to and watching the teacher, and copying what they hear and see. The aim is to internalise the sound before relating it to a symbol. (Reading notation is a means of preserving and making music, not an end in itself).

CD track 07 is designed so that every note in the relevant key can be played, which allows for progression within the activity.

TEACHING IN GROUPS

To begin with, the group can copy 2-bar phrases played by the teacher. At a later stage, students can take turns to improvise a 2-bar prompt, which can then be copied by the other players. This ensures that all students are engaged in the activities for the maximum amount of time.

Whilst the main focus of the activity is an aural one, teachers can nevertheless draw the attention of students to points of technique. For example, holding instruments properly and sitting or standing correctly.

DIFFERENTIATION

This activity can be performed by complete beginners, using just one or two notes. More notes can be introduced as students increase their range.

More advanced students may play phrases using any notes in the relevant key. Students can also pass an improvised 2-bar phrase around the group.

EXTENSION ACTIVITIES

Opportunities can be taken to create new musical games in order to develop students' short term memory. Players can be encouraged to devise these as the activity proceeds, building on prior learning. For example, the first player plays a rhythm on two or three notes, and another player repeats the rhythm but plays it on two different notes.

➡ 'Listen and Answer'; 'Instant Ensemble' .

Listen and Answer

EXPLORATIONS

- This listen and answer activity is for one or more players.

- Play each of the 2-bar phrases below. Each phrase should then be immediately answered by another player. *[CD07, CD08]*

- The 'answering' phrase should use notes and rhythms from the 'question' phrases.

EXAMPLE 2-BAR PHRASE

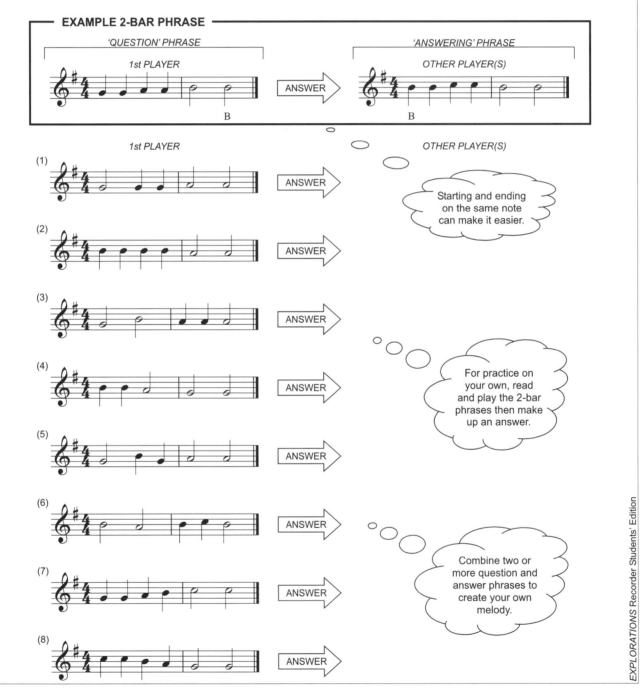

POINTS TO NOTE ON THE DVD

LISTEN AND ANSWER

- The teacher introduces the activity from the perspective of notation, by playing the given example at the top of the page with the student. It can also be introduced, however, without notation.

- As a practical reference point, she relates this 'Listen and Answer' activity on open strings to 'One-Note Rhythm Games', which the student has already played.

- The student copies the teacher's phrasing. The teacher moves on quickly to improvising on the scale because the student is technically beyond the 'open strings' stage. Notice the use of praise.

EXPLORATIONS Recorder Students' Edition

LEARNING OBJECTIVES

To improvise an 'answering' phrase to a rhythmic pattern played by the teacher (or heard on CD).

This 'Listen and Answer' activity can be introduced through clapping and singing. Singing a phrase before trying to play it encourages improvisation to be a head-led rather than a finger-led activity.

It can be helpful to assign 'word-rhythms' or French rhythm terms to note values. Examples of these are provided in the text for 'Listen and Copy', p.6.

When introducing the activity for the first time, students should be given the choice to either copy the 2-bar phrase played to them, or 'answer' it when they feel confident to do so.

Confidence can be encouraged by making improvisation a normal and usual part of the learning process, both in the practice room and at home.

Simulated performances in lessons of 'Listen and Copy' and 'Listen and Answer' can also be particularly beneficial in developing confidence.

HOMEWORK ACTIVITIES:

(1) 'Answer' the given phrases using CD track 08.

(2) Hum or sing a 2-bar phrase and then 'answer' it on the instrument accompanied by CD track 07.

BACKGROUND INFORMATION

This activity, sometimes known as 'call-and-response', builds upon the skills developed in ACTIVITY 3 of 'One-Note Rhythm Games'.

Improvisation offers opportunities for students to develop their own musical ideas within the context of what they have learned. As skills and knowledge improve, so should proficiency in improvisation. Improvisation helps musicians to acquire a deeper insight into musical styles and helps them to articulate their own feelings.

It should not, however, be perceived as a separate entity, but as an integral part of music learning. Improvisation can accelerate the acquisition of technique and help to develop related physical skills.

TEACHING IN GROUPS

To begin with, students can take turns to 'answer' a 2-bar phrase played by the teacher.

At a later stage, students may take turns to improvise a 2-bar 'question' phrase which can then be copied by the other members of the group. This ensures that all students are engaged in the activities for the maximum amount of time.

The teacher can take the opportunity to incorporate essential musical elements into the activity. For example playing legato or staccato, playing with dynamics, and/or introducing rests.

DIFFERENTIATION

This activity can be performed by complete beginners, using just one or two notes. More notes can be introduced as students increase their range.

More advanced students may play phrases using any notes in the relevant key. Students can also pass an improvised 2-bar phrase around the group.

EXTENSION ACTIVITIES

By improvising their own 2-bar 'question' phrases and then 'answering' them, students can gradually develop the skill of composing 4- and 8-bar melodies, using just 3 or 4 notes.

At a later stage, students can be encouraged to notate their improvisations. These may then be refined and developed into finished compositions.

➡ 'Word-Rhythms'; 'Staccato Starter'; 'Instant Ensemble'.

Pitch by Steps and Leaps

EXPLORATIONS

- This pitch activity is for one or more players.
- Using notes drawn from part of any scale or arpeggio, create short phrases by playing up and down the steps below (short steps can represent scalic movement, and deep ones can represent any interval).
- Lastly, combine steps and leaps to create your own composition.

(1)

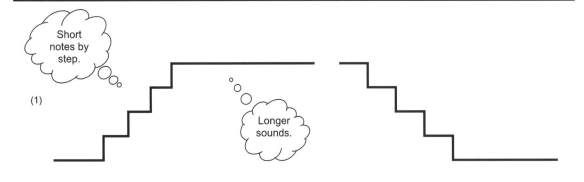

Short notes by step.

Longer sounds.

(2)

(3)

MY STEP-AND-LEAP COMPOSITION

EXPLORATIONS Recorder Students' Edition

POINTS TO NOTE ON THE DVD

PITCH BY STEPS AND LEAPS:

Please refer to examples of graphic score in DVD chapter **DOT-DASH PHRASES**.

LEARNING OBJECTIVES

To make links between sounds and symbols when interpreting a graphic score. For example, pitch and note length.

Students often require very little help in order to commence work on the activity, and this can result in a more spontaneous and personal interpretation.

However, the teacher should indicate which notes are to be used, and practise them with the students, before starting the activity.

By way of introduction, the teacher may play parts of the score and then ask students to identify them, or play and interpret one section in different ways.

Students might be encouraged to sing a phrase before attempting to play it. The teacher may use simple hand-signals to approximately indicate pitch and note lengths.

The score may be performed quiet, loud, fast, slow, high, low, slurred or legato, with a time signature or without; phrases can be played in any order, including retrograde and inverted interpretations.

Students can make a record of their interpretation/composition by adding letter-names to the steps.

HOMEWORK ACTIVITIES:

(1) Compose a short graphic score using a range of steps and leaps.

(2) Compose a descriptive graphic score. For example, to illustrate marching soldiers, a sunrise and sunset, a rocket blasting off into space, etc.

BACKGROUND INFORMATION

Composing with graphic score evolved during the 20th century and allows the performer(s) greater freedom in the choice of notes, time-scale and dynamics than is possible when using staff notation. The musical outcome is therefore more dependent upon the ideas, creativity and interpretation of the performers, who can subsequently lay a degree of claim to the ownership of the music.

Giving students the opportunity to work creatively with graphic scores supports the concept of 'relating sound to symbol'.

In the graphic scores opposite, students are encouraged to make relationships between pitch and note lengths by interpreting a graphical representation of a musical phrase.

TEACHING IN GROUPS

Students can work individually within the group in order to devise their own interpretation of a particular phrase. They can then each play their phrases to the whole group for comparison and discussion.

Alternatively, students may work together in twos or threes to produce a group performance, whilst the teacher ensures that every player has an opportunity to contribute fully.

As an aid to composing, students can refer to the 'Example Descriptive Titles' in the 'Dot-Dash Phrases' activity, if appropriate.

DIFFERENTIATION

Less experienced players can use a section of a simple scale, e.g. within the range of D to A. More advanced students may use a complete scale. For example, major, minor, whole-tone or chromatic.

EXTENSION ACTIVITIES

Further 'steps' and 'leaps' can be added to the score as students increase their playing range.

A story line, mood or feeling may be incorporated into the activity, and a title added.

A performance may be appropriate.

'Dot-Dash Phrases'; 'Matching Sound to Symbol'; 'A Sound-Effect Story'.   © Team World Music Ltd 2004

Play a Well-Known Tune 'By Ear'

Au Clair de la Lune *[CD09, CD10, CD11]*

G   G   G   A   B   A

Merrily We Roll Along *[CD12, CD13, CD14]*

B   A   G   A   B   B   B

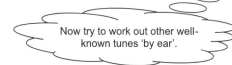
Now try to work out other well-known tunes 'by ear'.

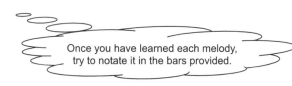
Once you have learned each melody, try to notate it in the bars provided.

Memorising (1)

┌─ **EXPLORATIONS** ───┐

- This memorising activity is for one or more players.

- Practise each tune in turn until performance standard is reached.

- Using the notation, try to memorise the first two bars, then look away and play them from memory.

- Apply this method to each subsequent 2-bar phrase so that the first 4 bars, then 6, then 8 can be performed without notation.

- Lastly, try memorising your favourite tunes using this technique.

└──┘

In the BAG!

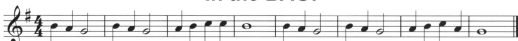

Call a CAB!

┌─ **POINTS TO NOTE ON THE DVD** ───────────────────────────────────┐

PLAY A WELL-KNOWN TUNE BY EAR: Please refer to DVD chapter **NAME THAT TUNE**.

MEMORISING (1)

- The teacher continually makes reference to the structure of the piece. For example, to the relationship between the 2-bar phrases. This is an aid to memorisation.

- Singing the letter-names of the piece encourages internalisation.

- Whilst the activity is approached from the standpoint of 'symbol to sound', the final, memorised performance clearly indicates that internalisation has been achieved.

└──┘

EXPLORATIONS Recorder Students' Edition

LEARNING OBJECTIVES

To work out 'by ear' how to play short, easy phrases from well-known tunes.

To start the activity, students should listen to a performance of the melody. This can be played by the teacher or played from the CD. The melody might then be sung to be sure that it has been correctly internalised. Students can use simple hand-signals to approximately indicate pitch and note lengths.

Playing 'by ear' almost always involves a degree of 'trial and error'. Some students may need reassuring that mistakes and corrections are a normal part of the learning process.

BACKGROUND INFORMATION

Like 'Listen and Copy' and 'Listen and Answer', playing 'by ear' is a basic technique of learning music in many cultures around the world.

Many students experiment with tunes they know before starting formal instrumental lessons, even when they have not been encouraged to do so. Playing 'by ear' in lessons encourages students to regard the activity as normal and acceptable, and promotes confidence.

TEACHING IN GROUPS

Students can work out tunes 'by ear' together, using a process of discussion and experimentation. This can be teacher- or student-led.

DIFFERENTIATION

More advanced students can be asked to work out the melodies one note higher. For example, in D major if the given example is in C major.

EXTENSION ACTIVITIES

Pieces of greater length and wider range may gradually be introduced.

LEARNING OBJECTIVES

To memorise with accuracy selected short, simple pieces.

When using the teaching strategies indicated, account should be taken of the various ways in which students memorise and internalise. Some will do it in terms of finger movements (kinaesthetic); others will remember the structure (visual); some will focus on the sound and musical line (aural).

Students may be asked to internalise each 2-bar phrase without playing it first. They may then look away and play it from memory.

BACKGROUND INFORMATION

Many students memorise music naturally, whilst others need more help and encouragement.

By memorising pieces, players are able to concentrate more closely on the music, and communicate more directly. Playing from memory is a realistic expectation of all students from beginner to advanced, and can be incorporated into regular lessons.

TEACHING IN GROUPS

During the lesson, students can be assigned individual phrases to learn from memory. These can then be performed in correct sequence. Students may then play their phrases to complete the entire melody.

DIFFERENTIATION

Less advanced students can learn, from memory, simple individual phrases. The teacher and pupil may then perform the melody together, the teacher completing the gaps within the melodic line. This creates a 'Listen and Copy/Answer' effect.

EXTENSION ACTIVITIES

Students can be asked to sing a melody from memory whilst performing the appropriate fingerings on their instruments.

➡ 'Name that Tune'; 'Memorising (2)'.

Word-Rhythms

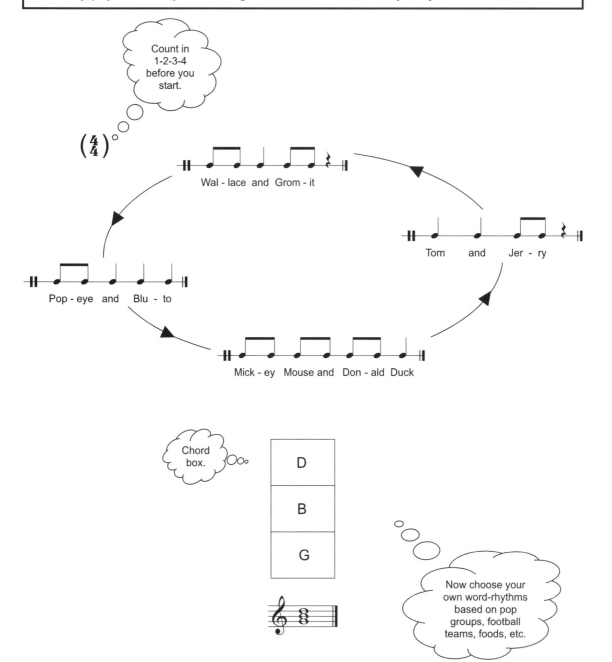

EXPLORATIONS Recorder Students' Edition

POINTS TO NOTE ON THE DVD

WORD-RHYTHMS:

Please refer to examples of 'Word-Rhythms' in DVD chapter **CARIBBEAN RHYTHM ROUND.**

LEARNING OBJECTIVES

To play with others, demonstrating some basic ensemble skills by listening, watching and keeping in time with the group; to distinguish between the elements of pulse, rhythm and tempo.

This activity can be introduced by speaking the 'word-rhythms' aloud, clapping or singing. Approaching the activity in this way can help students to internalise the relevant musical ideas before attempting to play them on their instruments.

When using the chord box, students may play the rhythms on any note, or alternate between any two or three notes. The activity can also be played throughout in 3-part harmony. The chord can be introduced separately. For example, as long notes, perhaps building up from the lowest note.

Students can be encouraged to explore their own 'word-rhythms', drawing upon known phrases or words. These can be linked to a different subject area, such as those given in the bubble opposite. If appropriate, the words and/or rhythms may be notated or recorded. They can be arranged in cyclic form.

HOMEWORK ACTIVITIES:

(1) Play the given 'word-rhythms' with CD track 15.

(2) Improvise new 'word-rhythms' accompanied by CD track 16.

BACKGROUND INFORMATION

By the time students attend their first instrumental lesson, they will have heard and sung hundreds of word-rhythms in nursery rhymes, hymns or other songs. This 'Word-Rhythms' activity teaches students to transfer such previously acquired knowledge onto an instrument in a creative and structured way.

It can also serve as an introduction to performing in an ensemble, playing in harmony, and learning about 'round' structure.

In the first instance, the activity separates the musical elements of pulse, rhythm, pitch and harmony. These can be brought together at a time that is appropriate for the students.

TEACHING IN GROUPS

Students can be asked to clap a 4-beat pulse whilst the teacher plays the rhythm, and vice-versa. Then, the students might clap the pulse whilst saying the 'word-rhythms'. The activity can also be played as a round.

'Word-Rhythms' can be of particular benefit to some students when they are first introduced to improvisation, and are easily incorporated into 'Listen and Copy' and 'Listen and Answer' activities. In this 'Word-Rhythms' activity, for example, one student can clap, say or play each of the rhythms in turn and the others copy.

At a later stage, students can take turns to make up a 'word-rhythm', and to clap, say or play it for the others to copy.

DIFFERENTIATION

Complete beginners can perform the activity using any note from the chord box which is easy for them to play.

More advanced players may choose to play any note from the relevant arpeggio or incorporate the added 6th or 7th, as appropriate.

EXTENSION ACTIVITIES

As students widen their playing range, other chords may be introduced. For example, the dominant and sub dominant chords.

Also, dissonant harmonies can be explored by, for example, improvising, using randomly selected chords.

➡ 'Make up a Song'; 'Sound-Scape'; 'Caribbean Rhythm Round'. © Team World Music Ltd 2004

Rhythm Grids

EXPLORATIONS

- These rhythm grids, for one or more players, can be clapped, sung or played on any note(s).
- Starting with the first grid, play each row from left to right, maintaining a 4-beat pulse throughout. *[CD17]*
- Then play the grids in different ways, for example, in unison, in rounds, and in harmony using notes from the chord boxes. *[CD17]*
- Each chord box lasts for one bar.

Count in
1-2-3-4.

You can play a
rhythm grid fast,
slow, high, low,
quiet or loud.

(1)

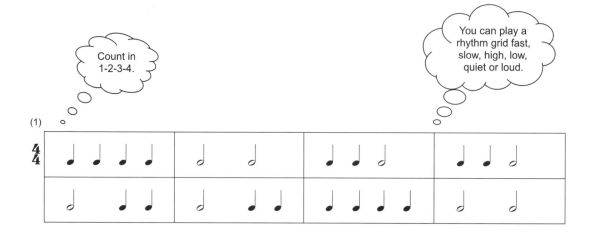

(2)

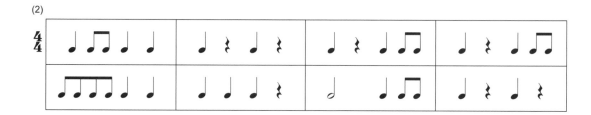

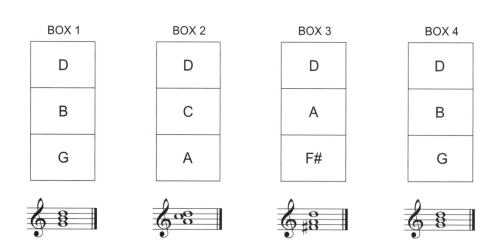

BOX 1   BOX 2   BOX 3   BOX 4

BOX 1	BOX 2	BOX 3	BOX 4
D	D	D	D
B	C	A	B
G	A	F#	G

POINTS TO NOTE ON THE DVD

RHYTHM GRIDS

- The activity is introduced with a firm pulse by the teacher.
- The chosen tonality of D major is related to a relevant examination scale, indicating an holistic approach.
- There is discussion about the phrasing of the improvisation.
- The teacher suggests that two other examination-related scales are applied to the activity for the next lesson.

LEARNING OBJECTIVES

To recognise and discriminate between the musical elements of pulse, rhythm, pitch, tempo, dynamics, texture, and notice changes of tone quality and colour.

These 'Rhythm Grids' activities can be introduced through clapping, speaking rhythms or singing, using different tempi and varied dynamics.

To begin, it can be helpful to assign 'word-rhythms' or French rhythm terms to note values. For example:

Alternatively, students may invent their own 'word-rhythms'. Before attempting to play them, students can clap a 4-beat pulse whilst the teacher plays the rhythm (and vice-versa).

The chords can be introduced separately as indicated. For example, long notes, perhaps building up from the lowest note. They may then be played as a 4-chord sequence, first as semibreves, as given, then as minims, and then as crotchets.

When the elements of rhythm and harmony are first combined, students can be advised to choose a simple sequence of four notes, selected from the given boxes. For example, G-A-A-D in the example opposite.

HOMEWORK ACTIVITIES:

All of the suggested activities can be practised and performed using CD track 17.

BACKGROUND INFORMATION

This 'Rhythm Grids' activity builds upon the skills developed in 'One-Note Rhythm Games' and 'Word-Rhythms'.

The activity is intended to help students to read staff notation by separating the musical elements of pulse, rhythm, pitch, tempo, texture and harmony.

The 'Rhythm Grids' can also be used as a compositional device and as a means of learning about and exploring harmony.

TEACHING IN GROUPS

When two or more students are present in the lesson, the 3-part harmony can be fully realised. It is recommended that the two elements of rhythm and harmony are separated until students are quite familiar with both.

Students can take turns to play a 2-bar phrase on a chosen note. This can then be expanded to two adjacent notes, and then three. For example, the first three notes of a scale. Students can be encouraged to listen to each others' phrases and to respond appropriately when taking their own turn.

In order to establish the concept of a 'group pulse', students can be asked to play the first two bars of a grid together (perhaps in harmony) and then to 'think silently' through the next two, and so on, alternately, to the end of the grid.

DIFFERENTIATION

When interpreting the rhythms prior to using the chord boxes, students may choose to play any note(s) that they are able to produce easily.

When drawing upon notes from the chord boxes students may choose to play notes that are easily produced on their instrument.

They can restrict their range of notes by moving step-wise until their playing range increases.

EXTENSION ACTIVITIES

When using the grids for composing, they might also be played diagonally, vertically or include a combination of rhythms from both grids. Students may also create their own chord boxes to produce different harmonic effects.

➡ 'A Rhythm Round'; 'Make up a Song'; 'Composing with Copy and Answer'. © Team World Music Ltd 2004

Staccato Starter

EXPLORATIONS

- This warm-up activity is for one or more players.
- Using any note of the given chord, play repeated staccato crotchets with the accompaniment. *[CD18]*
- Next, create different staccato rhythms, such as those illustrated, and perform with the accompaniment. *[CD18]*

REPEATED CROTCHETS

THE CHORD

EXAMPLE RHYTHMS

ACCOMPANIMENT

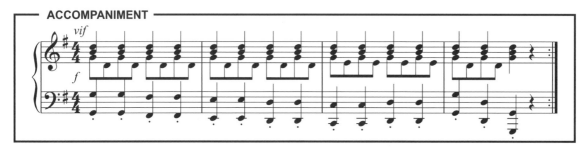

Create-a-Chord

EXPLORATIONS

- This warm-up activity is for three or more players.
- In your group, choose any note you know and hold it for several beats.
- At a given moment, change to a different note, or repeat your original note.
- Experiment creating sequences of chords, discussing the effects they produce.

EXAMPLE CHORDS

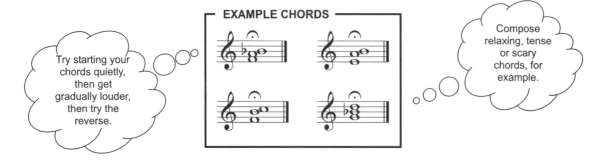

Try starting your chords quietly, then get gradually louder, then try the reverse.

Compose relaxing, tense or scary chords, for example.

EXPLORATIONS Recorder Students' Edition

POINTS TO NOTE ON THE DVD

STACCATO STARTER
- The students are asked to play the relevant scale before they are asked to decorate it.
- Students are given the opportunity to make up their own rhythm rather than being given one by the teacher.

CREATE-A-CHORD
- The teacher introduces the activity by asking the students to choose and play any notes.
- There is a discussion on harmonic and dissonant chords and their effects or moods.
- Students then choose ways of transforming the result into a piece of music by selecting differing kinds of phrases in distinct styles. The outcome indicates that the students are musically engaged throughout.

LEARNING OBJECTIVES

To improvise short, easy staccato patterns and then repeat them from memory.

The teacher can demonstrate 'Staccato Starter' by playing the given examples and describing the activity.

Students can then be asked to play a row of seven staccato crotchets on any one note, then repeat it. Next, students can change one or more of the staccato crotchets into a pair of quavers. The activity can be extended by using two notes, playing crotchets and quavers, as in the first example rhythm.

HOMEWORK ACTIVITIES:

Experiment with improvising 2-bar phrases accompanied by CD track 18.

BACKGROUND INFORMATION

This activity builds upon the aural and technical skills developed in 'Listen and Copy', 'Listen and Answer', and 'Word-Rhythms'.

In 'Staccato Starter', however, the student is required to remember exactly what notes and rhythms they have played and immediately repeat them.

The limited number of notes in the arpeggio, from which the students can choose, increases their chance of completing the activity successfully. The chord also provides a group of students with the opportunity to play in harmony.

TEACHING IN GROUPS

Students can take turns to improvise a 2-bar phrase which they then repeat, whilst the others in the group repeat the given rhythm on their own choice of notes.

DIFFERENTIATION

Less advanced players can use any one or two notes whilst the more advanced can use an extended arpeggio.

EXTENSION ACTIVITIES

Improvise a 2-bar phrase then repeat it by singing from memory and vice-versa.

LEARNING OBJECTIVES

To create a tone-cluster composition with others, demonstrating basic ensemble skills of listening, watching and playing as an independent part in the texture.

The example chords may be played and discussed if appropriate. Otherwise, proceed as indicated on the tutorial page.

Players can be asked to volunteer to lead the group, by using appropriate eye contact and body movements.

Students should be able to name any note(s) they have played. This ensures that they are developing a sense of aural and technical control within the activity.

BACKGROUND INFORMATION

Most students, even quite young ones, are familiar with dissonant harmonies through the media of film and television.

This 'Create-a-Chord' activity can be used to compose a group piece based on a mood, scene or event. Alternatively, students may be asked to find a poem or story that can be musically illustrated with tone-clusters.

TEACHING IN GROUPS

Players could make their entries at, for example, 4-second intervals so that the chord is continuously changing.

The 'lead' player might then begin to introduce a rhythm at the start of each long note. For example:

DIFFERENTIATION

The activity allows complete beginners to compose with very advanced players.

➡ 'A Rhythm Round'; 'Sound-Scape'.

Dot-Dash Phrases

EXPLORATIONS

- This activity is for one or more players.

- First, learn to play the given scale, with and without notation.

- Starting on any note of the given scale, play the phrases by interpreting the dot-and-dash symbols (dots represent short sounds, and dashes represent long).

- Then perform 'Hopscotch' which combines dot-dash phrases.

- Lastly, using the given phrases and example titles below, compose your own piece of descriptive music. Notate your composition in the box provided.

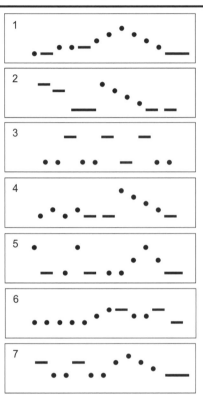

SCALE OF F

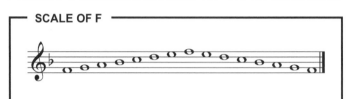

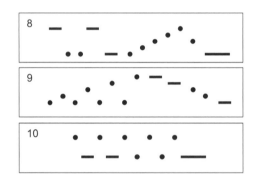

EXAMPLE DESCRIPTIVE TITLES

'JUMPING BEANS'   'SPACE-WALK'

'TRAMPOLINING'   'THE TRAFFIC JAM'

'THE HARE AND THE TORTOISE'

HOPSCOTCH

MY DOT-DASH COMPOSITION

POINTS TO NOTE ON THE DVD

DOT-DASH PHRASES

- Students play the scale in order to establish a familiar tonality for the activity. The teacher then interprets a phrase and asks students to identify it.

- The first two students each interpret a phrase, the second of which is in triple time. The third student is not given this opportunity, and subsequently has difficulties in 'Hopscotch'.

- There are discussions about 'structure', about 'how to improve the activity' and about 'what is expected in the next lesson'.

LEARNING OBJECTIVES

To compose a piece of music through the medium of a graphic score, making links between the sounds and symbols.

The teacher might start the activity by playing some of the phrases and then asking students to identify them. Alternatively, one phrase might be performed in many different ways. For example, starting on a higher or lower note, playing quiet or loud, fast or slow, legato or staccato. Students may experiment with various time signatures, or interpret phrases 'freely'.

Players can be shown how to extend a phrase by applying the compositional techniques of imitation, sequence or retrograde to a second playing of the phrase, as exemplified on pp. 26, 27 and 32. They might also combine phrases to devise more complex structures. For example, A-B-B-A form.

The teacher may indicate the relationship between one of the phrases and an 'example descriptive title'. For example, phrase 3 and 'Jumping Beans'.

HOMEWORK ACTIVITIES:

(1) Compose a 'Dot-Dash' piece and notate it by adding letter-names.

(2) Prepare a performance of the piece with expression, trying to reflect the subject matter and/or mood of the title.

BACKGROUND INFORMATION

This 'Dot-Dash Phrases' activity, like all compositional work, helps students to explore music 'from the inside'.

Composing is valuable in its own right, but it can also be used to develop performing skills, knowledge and understanding.

The teacher can promote confidence by demonstrating how to experiment with the 'Dot-Dash Phrases', and by providing step by step assistance with models, patterns and procedures.

The open-ended nature of the activity can be emphasised - all outcomes are valued and enjoyed.

TEACHING IN GROUPS

Students can work individually within the group in order to compose their own interpretation of a particular phrase. They can then each play their phrase to the whole group for comparison and discussion.

Alternatively, students may work together in twos or threes to produce a group performance, whilst the teacher ensures that every player has an opportunity to contribute fully.

Some of the 'Example Descriptive Titles' may suggest a group composition. For example, 'The Traffic Jam' and 'The Hare and the Tortoise'.

DIFFERENTIATION

All of the phrases can be played by students who have a playing range of at least six notes.

This allows for the possibility of discovering 'sequence', and exploring tonic and supertonic tonalities. More advanced students can use the complete scale, adding higher or lower notes if desired, as well as incorporating some chromaticism.

EXTENSION ACTIVITIES

More advanced students can be encouraged to transfer their phrases/composition into staff notation.

All students can be asked to devise their own descriptive titles and to compose pieces based upon them.

'Matching Sound to Symbol'; 'Make up a Song'; 'Tell a Story with Music'.   © Team World Music Ltd 2004

A Rhythm Round

EXPLORATIONS

- This rhythm round, for two or more players, can be clapped, sung, or played on any note(s).

- Practise the rhythm, then play it as a round or in unison, or in harmony using notes from the chord boxes below. *[CD19]*

- Each chord box lasts for one bar.

BOX 1	BOX 2	BOX 3	BOX 4
C	D	C	C
A	Bb	Bb	A
F	F	G	F

You could play your rhythm round fast, slow, high, low, loud or quiet on any instruments, or voice and clapping!

POINTS TO NOTE ON THE DVD

A RHYTHM ROUND:

Please refer to examples of rhythm work in DVD chapter **CARIBBEAN RHYTHM ROUND**.

LEARNING OBJECTIVES

To play with others, demonstrating some basic ensemble skills by listening, watching and keeping time with the group.

As with previous related activities, the 'Rhythm Round' can be introduced through clapping, speaking rhythms or singing. Using word-rhythms might also be appropriate.

If students are already familiar with minims and crotchets, then the CD track 19 can be used at the very start of the activity. One approach, for example, is to direct the students to clap the round in unison and then as a round, with the accompaniment. Students can then play through the round on their instruments, using any note directed by the teacher, without accompaniment.

The chords can be introduced separately, perhaps building up from the lowest note. Students could then repeat lines (1) and (2) on their instruments, starting on any note in the first chord box. They may then move, by step, to a different note selected from subsequent boxes. Remember that each chord box lasts for one bar. A complete performance of 'A Rhythm Round' could be attempted, first without, and then with the accompaniment.

HOMEWORK ACTIVITIES:

Students can practise the round by choosing different selections of notes from the chord boxes, accompanied by the CD.

BACKGROUND INFORMATION

Rounds are one of the most traditional forms of music-making in Western culture.

This 'Rhythm Round' activity builds upon the knowledge and skills developed in 'Rhythm Grids', and helps students to read staff notation by separating the musical elements of rhythm, pitch, pulse, tempo and texture.

Practising and performing rounds, which are pieces of extended length, can help to build up stamina.

TEACHING IN GROUPS

When two or more students are present in the lesson, the 3-part harmony can be fully realised. It is recommended that the two elements of rhythm and harmony are separated until students are quite familiar with both.

The 'teaching in groups' strategies suggested for 'Rhythm Grids' can also be applied to this activity.

When performing the 'Rhythm Round' in its final, harmonised version, the teacher and students can discuss ways of improving and enhancing the activity. For example, by introducing dynamics in a variety of ways, by playing legato or staccato, or by converting some of the crotchets into pairs of quavers, or dotted crotchets followed by quavers.

Each student can be assigned a line of the 'Rhythm Round' to set to words. This could be undertaken within a chosen subject setting. For example, foods or sports.

DIFFERENTIATION

When moving from one chord box to the next, less experienced students may limit the notes they use. For example, they could simply alternate between any two adjacent notes. Advanced students can be encouraged to draw upon all of the notes in a chord box and, possibly, to transpose lower notes up an octave.

EXTENSION ACTIVITIES

Students can be asked to compose their own rhythm sequences, and then apply the chords from the chord boxes. Sequences may be developed by the inclusion of quavers and/or dotted notes, and possibly by the addition of words.

➡ 'Caribbean Rhythm Round'.

Matching Sound to Symbol

EXPLORATIONS

- This activity gives the opportunity to interpret symbols in a creative way.
- Using notes of your own choice, play through all the symbols below, then find ways of interpreting the graphic score.
- Finally, compose your own piece, notating it using the suggested symbols.

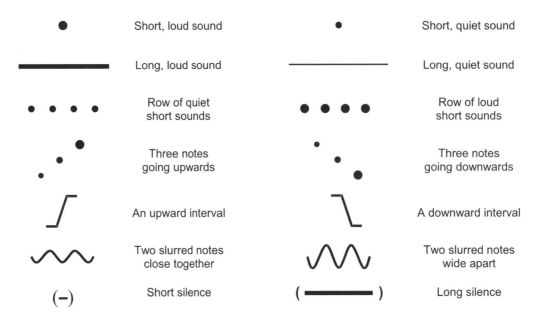

●	Short, loud sound	•	Short, quiet sound
▬▬▬	Long, loud sound	───	Long, quiet sound
● ● ● ●	Row of quiet short sounds	● ● ● ●	Row of loud short sounds
	Three notes going upwards		Three notes going downwards
	An upward interval		A downward interval
	Two slurred notes close together		Two slurred notes wide apart
(–)	Short silence	(▬▬▬)	Long silence

GRAPHIC SCORE

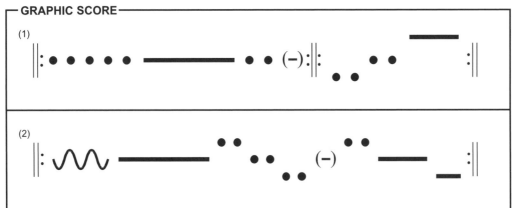

(1)

(2)

MY OWN COMPOSITION

EXPLORATIONS Recorder Students' Edition

POINTS TO NOTE ON THE DVD

MATCHING SOUND TO SYMBOL:

Please refer to examples of graphic score in DVD chapter **DOT-DASH PHRASES**.

'Matching Sound to Symbol' is an activity for one or more players. The teacher might introduce the activity by interpreting some of the symbols with the student(s).

Whilst initially interpreting the symbols, the teacher can lead a discussion on the open-ended nature of the activity by posing relevant questions. For example:

(1) When the terms 'long' and 'short' are used, do they have exact meanings?

(2) Do 'upward' and 'downward' intervals have to be wide or narrow?

(3) In the score, do the repeat marks mean that the repeated phrase should be played exactly like the first phrase?

(4) What is the importance of silence in the interpretation?

Any discussion on the interpretation of symbols can be supported by the teacher and/or students playing examples.

In performance, the graphic score may be enhanced by 'atmospheric' accompaniments available on CD tracks 54, 68 or 69.

HOMEWORK ACTIVITIES:

(1) Students can be asked to interpret the graphic score in two or more ways, perhaps to evoke different moods or feelings.

(2) Students can be given the task of composing pieces using graphic score, based upon descriptive ideas. For example, winter, space etc.

BACKGROUND INFORMATION

This graphic score activity emphasises the importance of making clear distinctions between loud and quiet, long and short, wide or close intervals, and sound and silence.

At the earliest stage, students should be encouraged to make expressive, musical decisions, either instinctively, or by evaluating and revising their work.

Whether using staff notation or graphic score, interpretation is the creative dimension of performing.

TEACHING IN GROUPS

Two or three students can experiment with exploring sounds to match the symbols. They might compare sounds and discuss changes and improvements.

When working together to interpret the graphic score, the performance of the individual sections can be divided between the players. For example, one student might play each phrase the first time, and another play the repeats. Letter-names might be inserted to avoid confusion between players.

When composing with graphic notation, the group can either produce individual compositions, work in pairs or compose a whole group piece. In whole group work, all players should be given the opportunity to provide input, discuss ideas and perform the musical outcome.

DIFFERENTIATION

Both the symbols and the graphic score offer infinite possibilities relating to pitch, note-length, dynamics, tempo, intervals and expression. This allows elementary students to play alongside advanced players. It also means that the activity can be revisited at different stages during the students' course.

EXTENSION ACTIVITIES

Students can be encouraged to make up their own sounds and to devise symbols to represent them. They may also be offered a selection of 'moods' and 'feelings' to express with the aid of a graphic score.

➡ 'A Sound-Effect Story'; 'Sound-Scape'; 'Tell a Story with Music'.

Jazz on 3 Notes

EXPLORATIONS

- This 12-bar blues activity is for one or more players.

- Learn 'Blue Triangle' *[CD20]*, then take turns to improvise using 2- and 4-bar phrases, drawing on notes and rhythms from the theme. *[CD21]*

- Finally, perform 'Blue Triangle', with improvised solos, playing the theme twice at the beginning and once at the end. *[CD22]*

THE 3 NOTES

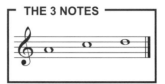

Blue Triangle
(Jazz theme)

EXAMPLE 2- & 4-BAR IMPROVISATIONS

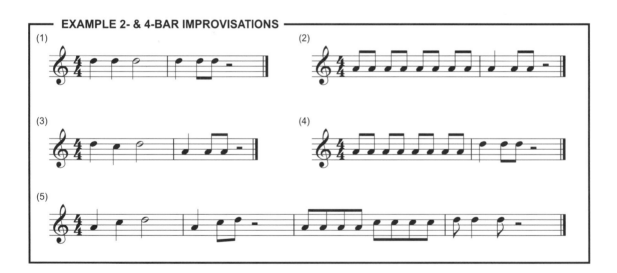

12-BAR BLUES ACCOMPANIMENT

D⁷	G⁷	D⁷	D⁷	G⁷	G⁷	D⁷	D⁷	Em⁷	A⁷	D⁷	D⁷

EXPLORATIONS Recorder Students' Edition

POINTS TO NOTE ON THE DVD

JAZZ ON 3 NOTES

- The teacher starts by performing 'Blue Triangle', then asks the band to sing it, so that it is internalised aurally.

- Some children seem to use the notation, whilst others appear comfortable without it.

- When the less experienced players vary the pulse, the accompanist adjusts accordingly.

- A teacher demonstrates how the melody may be simplified for less advanced students. Nevertheless, a violinist adopts a fast, aggressive bowing style in 12/8 time, quickly moving to a smooth legato technique. (The teacher may support the sound development of techniques that are discovered whilst improvising).

LEARNING OBJECTIVES

To improvise rhythmic and melodic phrases freely or within given structures, individually or as part of a group.

The 'Blue Triangle' theme can be clapped, sung or spoken in jazz rhythms (e.g. 'Do-do-dah'), before being played on an instrument.

The 'Blue Triangle' theme consists of three repeated 4-bar phrases and may be taught and learned aurally, prior to using the notation, or without reference to the notation, if desired.

Track 20 on the CD exemplifies the jazz rhythms that are a characteristic feature of 'Blue Triangle'.

Students should be advised to use only the three given notes when beginning to improvise. This ensures that they do not play any 'wrong' notes.

In the first instance, students may improvise on just one of the three notes (examples 1&2) then gradually extend the activity to two, and then three notes. The teaching techniques outlined in 'Listen and Copy/Answer' may be incorporated into the improvisation activity, supported by CD track 21.

HOMEWORK ACTIVITIES:

(1) Practise the 'Blue Triangle' theme accompanied by CD track 20.
(2) Experiment with improvisation with track 21.
(3) Attempt a complete performance with CD track 22, incorporating improvisations extended to 12 bars.

BACKGROUND INFORMATION

This activity teaches students how to improvise phrases with a limited choice of notes over a 12-bar blues chord sequence. The three notes used, A, C and D (bracketed), are derived from the 'blues' scale on D.

The notes F, G# and C are known as 'blue' notes because they do not belong to the tonality of D major (see 12-bar blues accompaniment).

TEACHING IN GROUPS

Within a group context, students can approach improvisation in a variety of ways. Some will internalise the three notes as an aural pattern and improvise without the notation whilst others may want to refer to the notation and interpret it in the jazz idiom. Other students may cognize in terms of finger movements, and so on. The teacher can help to ensure that each approach is acceptable, and students may vary their approach when interacting with others.

At a later stage, players can be encouraged to improvise at the same time, either by overlapping phrases, or by one player interpolating short phrases into the longer phrases of others.

DIFFERENTIATION

Complete beginners can improvise on any one or two of the given three notes, whereas more advanced players may use any number of relevant notes from the scale, including octave transpositions.

EXTENSION ACTIVITIES

Teachers may gradually introduce higher or lower notes adjacent to the ones given, so that students increase the range of their improvisation. Students can be encouraged to make up their own rhythmic patterns, as well as drawing upon those in 'Blue Triangle'.

➡ 'Blues Booster'; 'Dorian Jazz'.

A Sound-Effect Story

EXPLORATIONS

- This descriptive music activity is for two or more players.

- Using various instruments, experiment making sound-effects to match the symbols in the boxes below.

- Next, make up a story which could be illustrated with your sound-effects (you may wish to continue the example story).

- Lastly, perform your sound-effect story, with or without a narrator.

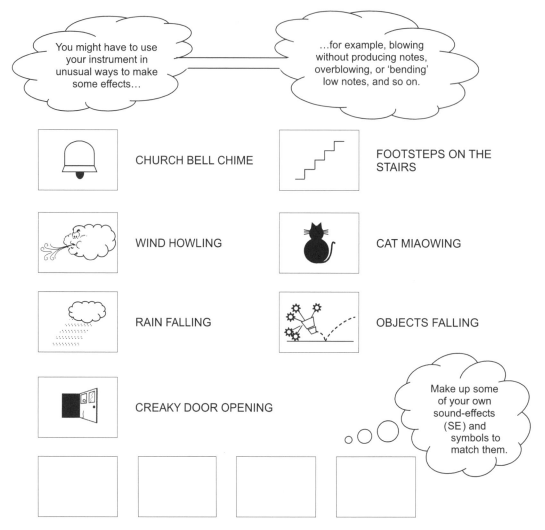

You might have to use your instrument in unusual ways to make some effects…

…for example, blowing without producing notes, overblowing, or 'bending' low notes, and so on.

CHURCH BELL CHIME

FOOTSTEPS ON THE STAIRS

WIND HOWLING

CAT MIAOWING

RAIN FALLING

OBJECTS FALLING

CREAKY DOOR OPENING

Make up some of your own sound-effects (SE) and symbols to match them.

EXAMPLE SOUND-EFFECT STORY

"I don't know why I went up to the old house that night. They said it was haunted, but I never believed them. But I must admit, I sure felt a bit uneasy that night.

The wind howled (SE). The rain lashed down (SE). And for some unknown reason, the church bell struck one (SE) even though it was only ten! Anyway, I…(etc)"

EXPLORATIONS Recorder Students' Edition

POINTS TO NOTE ON THE DVD

A SOUND-EFFECT STORY

- The teacher introduces and demonstrates sound-effects, and leads a discussion on the various component parts of 'Wind'. For example, it is not just 'one sound'.

- A student uses the word 'moaning', and suggests using low F#. He discovers that harmonics can 'bend'.

- The effects all require deep breaths and sustained blowing, which can be related to other parts of the lesson.

- The 'water-key' sound-effect technique is related to the key's orthodox function.

LEARNING OBJECTIVES

To hear sounds in the environment internally, and to replicate them on instruments 'illustrating' a story with sound.

Like 'Matching Sound to Symbol', and 'Pitch by Steps and Leaps', this activity can be mostly 'student-led'.

To begin, students can be asked to hear a specific sound in their heads (e.g. a church bell chime), and discuss how this might be best achieved. Students may then try various ways of producing the effect on their instruments. Sometimes, students discover specific aspects of technique through these activities. For example, 'sforzando', flutter-tonguing on woodwind instruments, 'col legno' on strings, or pedal notes on brass.

As an alternative to using only sound-effects to illustrate a story, students can also incorporate evocative, melodic phrases, using the skills developed in 'Matching Sound to Symbol' and 'Dot-Dash Phrases'.

If the suggested story-line is used, the sound-effects may be supported by the 'atmospheric' accompaniments available on CD tracks 54, 68 or 69.

HOMEWORK ACTIVITIES:

Play a selection of sound-effects, or evocative phrases, accompanied by CD tracks 54, 68 or 69.

BACKGROUND INFORMATION

Composers from all periods have used instruments and voices to create sound-effects, from Medieval through to Modern times.

A few well-known examples include references to bird-song by Beethoven, Respighi, Delius and Messiaen, ships' engines by Elgar, and the percussion 'gunfight' in Copland's 'Billy the Kid' Suite.

Such effects are always handled sensitively and expressively by composers, and the same, serious approach should be encouraged when students are engaging in this activity.

TEACHING IN GROUPS

Students can use varying devices within the group to produce effects. For example, whilst one is playing the instrument, another might play on the mouthpiece and another play 'muted'. In mixed lessons, effects can be instrument specific because of the facilities of wider range, pizzicato, flutter-tonguing, etc.

Alternatively, there may be instances where all players do the same thing. For example, sing or blow air through the instruments to suggest the sound of the wind.

The group activity can be enhanced by incorporating a wider range of instruments, e.g. any combination of brass, woodwind, strings and percussion. This can be achieved by liaising with and working alongside a classroom music teacher and/or other instrumental teachers.

DIFFERENTIATION

Many sounds are not essentially dependent upon 'orthodox technique', so the activity offers virtually infinite differentiation.

For this reason, it is recommended that students are not introduced to these activities very early in their course. This will ensure that they do not acquire unorthodox playing techniques, such as 'false embouchure' on brass instruments, for example.

EXTENSION ACTIVITIES

Students can be asked to create their own sound-effects and to create a story around them. Conversely, they can write a story, poem or script, and create sound-effects to illustrate them.

➡ 'Sound-Scape'; 'Tell a Story with Music'.

Pent-Up Blues

EXPLORATIONS

- This blues improvising activity is for one or more players.

- First, memorise the A minor pentatonic scale.

- Next, learn bars 2, 4, 6, 8, 9 and 10 and practise these with the CD or with your teacher playing the accompaniment.

- Then try improvising your own melodic 'fills' for these bars using the A minor pentatonic scale.

- Finally, perform Pent Up Blues, playing it firstly as written, then with your improvisations. More experienced players may play the power chords or bass notes.

A MINOR PENTATONIC SCALE

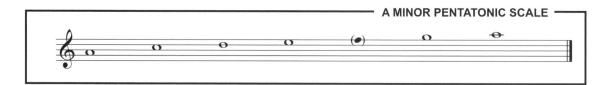

Pent-Up Blues

Leo Turner

POWER CHORDS

EXPLORATIONS Classical Guitar Students' Edition

POINTS TO NOTE ON THE DVD

PENT-UP BLUES:

Please refer to DVD chapter **JAZZ ON 3 NOTES**.

LEARNING OBJECTIVES

To improvise rhythmic and melodic phrases freely or within given structures, individually or as part of a group.

In order to place 'Pent-Up Blues' into its stylistic context, the teacher may consider performing the activity to the students. Students can benefit from clapping, speaking or singing the phrases at the same time, as a means of internalising.

All of the phrases in 'Pent-Up Blues' can be taught aurally if desired. If notation is then introduced, the teacher can draw students' attention to the use of tied notes, which consist of one sound but three symbols.

In the first instance, students may improvise on one of the notes, for example 'A', then gradually extend the activity to two, then three, and so on. The teaching techniques of 'Listen and Copy' and 'Listen and Answer' can be incorporated into the improvisation activity.

HOMEWORK ACTIVITIES:

(1) Learn to play 'Pent-Up Blues'.

(2) Experiment with improvisation.

(3) Play a complete performance of the activity.

BACKGROUND INFORMATION

This activity builds upon the skills learned in 'Jazz on 3 Notes'. The activity teaches students how to improvise phrases over a 12-bar blues chord sequence, using a limited number of notes.

However, the overall musical focus of this activity is 'blues-rock' rather than 'jazz'. This is because of the inclusion of 'power chords', a device used by many blues and rock guitarists.

'Power chords' are based on root, fifth and octave and therefore may be used in place of either major or minor chords. This simplifies the harmonic texture and can help to create an accompaniment with 'drive' and 'purpose'.

A solid 4-beat pulse should be maintained throughout.

GROUP TEACHING STRATEGIES

All students can be asked to play the 'on-beat' low notes in the odd-numbered bars while the teacher plays the higher phrases. At a later stage, this process can be reversed.

Students may then start to alternate solos with the teacher and with each other as well as taking turns to play the accompaniment.

At a later stage, players can be encouraged to improvise at the same time, either by overlapping phrases, or by interpolating short phrases into longer ones.

DIFFERENTIATION

Beginners can improvise on any one or two of the given five notes, whereas more advanced players may use any number of relevant notes from the given scale. The power chords offer a further challenge.

EXTENSION ACTIVITIES

Teachers may gradually introduce higher or lower notes adjacent to the ones given, so that students increase their range of improvisation. This may be done by the usual method of learning the scales 'positionally', and internalisation may be encouraged by asking students to play the scale on one string. Students can be encouraged to make up their own rhythmic patterns as well as drawing upon those in 'Pent-Up Blues'.

➡ 'Dorian Jazz', p.38.

Listen, Copy and Answer (1)

EXPLORATIONS

- This listen, copy and answer activity is for one or more players.
- Play each of the 2-bar phrases below. Each phrase should then be immediately copied or answered by another player. *[CD23 - 26]*
- The 'answering' phrases should use notes and rhythms from the question phrases.
- This activity can be performed using the example keyboard accompaniment. *[CD23 - 26]*

Start with LISTENING & COPYING…

…then move on to LISTENING & ANSWERING.

(1) *[CD23, CD24]*
Gently flowing
mf

(2)
Gently flowing
mf

(3)
mf

(4)
mf
(FOUR FURTHER 2-BAR EXAMPLES GIVEN ON CD)

(5) *[CD25, CD26]*
Gently flowing
mf

(6)
Gently flowing
mf

(7)
mf

(8)
mf
(FOUR FURTHER 2-BAR EXAMPLES GIVEN ON CD)

EXAMPLE ACCOMPANIMENT

Gently Flowing
mp

mp

G   G⁶   GMaj⁷   G⁶   G   G⁶   GMaj⁷   G⁶

POINTS TO NOTE ON THE DVD

LISTEN, COPY AND ANSWER (1)

- The teacher devises his own style of accompaniment for this diatonic improvisation scenario, rather than using the printed version (above).
- The students are offered effective modelling by the teacher before attempting the activity on their own.
- The improvised phrases played by the students are rhythmically interesting and are performed with musicianship, sensitivity and confidence.

LEARNING OBJECTIVES

To repeat with accuracy short, easy rhythmic and melodic phrases by playing back from memory; to improvise rhythmic and melodic phrases freely, or within given structures, individually or as part of a group.

Students should be familiar with at least the first five notes of the relevant scale when starting this activity.

In the first instance, students may find it easier to copy and 'answer' phrases that move in scales or arpeggios, as in the given examples. This can be done using just two or three notes in the first lesson, expanding to four or five in subsequent lessons.

When introducing 'Listen, Copy and Answer' for the first time in this key, students should be given the choice to either copy the 2-bar phrase, or to 'answer' it when they feel confident to do so.

At a later stage, the accompaniments on CD tracks 24 and 26 can be used for improvising completely original phrases, without reference to those given.

HOMEWORK ACTIVITIES:

(1) Copy and 'answer' the 2-bar phrases given on CD tracks 23 and 25.

(2) Improvise 2-bar phrases with CD tracks 24 and 26 and either repeat them or play an 'answer'.

BACKGROUND INFORMATION

This activity builds upon the knowledge and skills developed in 'Listen and Copy' and 'Listen and Answer'.

The 'Listen and Copy' form of the activity is very similar to one of the aural tests set by some examination boards. Here, students are offered the opportunity to repeat the given examples on their instruments, rather than to sing.

If preferred, teachers may introduce students to 'Instant Ensemble' before 'Listen, Copy and Answer (1)', if appropriate, because it provides a greater number of prompts in duple time and triple time is not introduced. Less advanced students may find this easier.

TEACHING IN GROUPS

To begin with, the group can copy 2-bar phrases played by the teacher, or by each of the students in turn.

At a later stage, the teacher and students may take turns to improvise 2-bar prompts, which can then be 'answered' individually by other students in the group. This ensures that all students are engaged in the activities for the maximum amount of time.

Interpretation is a dynamic and important ingredient of improvisation, and in this activity students should be encouraged to listen with focus and to 'answer' one anothers' improvisations expressively.

As students improve their ability to improvise, their musical awareness and fluency should develop also.

DIFFERENTIATION

The CD tracks 23-26 are designed so that improvisations can incorporate all of the notes in the key of F major (concert). This allows the teacher to play 2-bar prompts to students at varying stages of progress within this key. The teacher may refer more advanced students to the complete scale before starting the activity.

EXTENSION ACTIVITIES

Students can be asked to sing an improvisation whilst fingering the appropriate notes on their instruments.

By improvising their own 2-bar 'question' phrases and then 'answering' them, students can gradually develop the skill of composing 4- and 8-bar melodies.

➡ 'Instant Ensemble'; 'Chinese Music'; 'Composing with Copy and Answer'. © Team World Music Ltd 2004

Make Up a Song

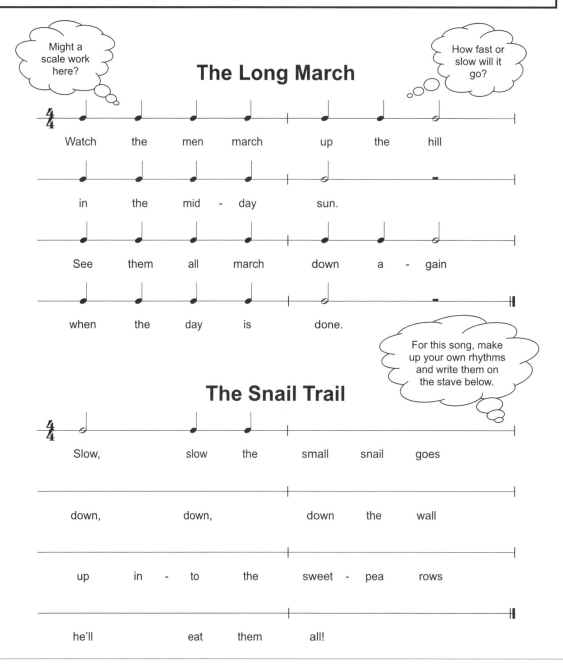

The Long March

Might a scale work here?

How fast or slow will it go?

Watch the men march up the hill

in the mid - day sun.

See them all march down a - gain

when the day is done.

The Snail Trail

For this song, make up your own rhythms and write them on the stave below.

Slow, slow the small snail goes

down, down, down the wall

up in - to the sweet - pea rows

he'll eat them all!

EXPLORATIONS Recorder Students' Edition

┌─ **POINTS TO NOTE ON THE DVD** ────────────────────────────────┐

MAKE UP A SONG

- The student is given the choice to select an appropriate tonality for the song, and is asked to justify his choice.

- There is a discussion about the mood of the words and how this could be portrayed musically. The student talks about the picture of the snail 'in his head', indicating internalisation.

- The student is fully engaged in the activity and plays with feeling and meaning.

└──┘

LEARNING OBJECTIVES

To compose, by developing musical ideas within given, simple structures, and applying instrumental skills.

This activity, like many others in the EXPLORATIONS series, often requires very little initial input by the teacher, and this can result in a greater feeling of involvement and ownership by students. If necessary, the first song activity, 'The Long March', can be used to model the composing process. Students can then work independently on 'The Snail Trail'. A variety of approaches to each song can be adopted. In the first instance students may sing improvised phrases using ascending and descending hand-signals to indicate the shape and structure of the verse. They can improvise freely, internalising the text while they do so. Students may record their work using 'dot-dash phrases' and letter names rather than notation.

The teacher can advise on phrase structure by bringing students' attention to compositional devices like imitation and sequence.

Technical suggestions might also be made. For example, would slurring most of a verse be more appropriate than tonguing? Could a mute be used to advantage?

HOMEWORK ACTIVITIES:

Students can be asked to write another verse for their song, or to explore verse/chorus form.

BACKGROUND INFORMATION

This activity builds upon several other related activities, especially 'Word-Rhythms', and 'Dot-Dash Phrases'.

Whilst composing songs might usually be associated with classroom music, instrumental lessons can present opportunities for students to extend ideas that start in classroom lessons. Instrumental teachers have a special expertise that helps students to explore the technical and expressive characteristics of the instrument through composing.

Setting words to music has been a component of some theory examinations over many years. Here, however, students are given the opportunity to compose a song through the medium of a musical instrument.

TEACHING IN GROUPS

Following the activity intructions (opposite), two or three students who like working together can co-operate at each stage of the composing process to create a song.

Students can bring their own, individual strengths to the activity. For example, by composing more verses or a chorus, suggesting a suitable accompaniment, perhaps with drones or an ostinato, evaluating and refining the song, or leading a group performance.

The teacher can ensure that all players have an opportunity to contribute.

DIFFERENTIATION

Less advanced students can restrict the range of their song and perhaps rely on simple ascending and descending patterns. More advanced players can be encouraged to use a greater range of notes on their instruments and to consider carefully the musical elements of dynamics, articulation, etc.

EXTENSION ACTIVITIES

Students can be asked to find a poem that interests them and set it to music. Alternatively, they might compose a melody, and then set words to it on any subject that interests them.

'Composing with Copy and Answer'; 'Songs of Persuasion'.

Name That Tune

EXPLORATIONS

- Taking each tune in turn, play or sing the 2-bar prompt and identify it.

- Then try to complete the melody 'by ear', listening carefully to whether each note is higher, lower, longer or shorter than the previous.

- Practise slowly and methodically, correcting mistakes, repeating phrases as appropriate, until you can play the entire melody.

- Once you have learned each melody, try to notate it in the bars provided. *[CD27 – CD32]*

Slowly [CD27, CD28, CD29]

Quickly [CD30, CD31, CD32]

Memorising (2)

EXPLORATIONS

- Practise each line in turn until performance standard is reached.

- Using the notation, try to memorise the first two bars, then look away and play them from memory.

- Apply this method to each subsequent 2-bar phrase so that the first 4 bars, then 6, then 8 can be performed without notation.

- Lastly, try memorising your favourite tunes using this technique.

Lively ⌢ *Fine*

D.C. al Fine

EXPLORATIONS Recorder Students' Edition

POINTS TO NOTE ON THE DVD

NAME THAT TUNE
- The teacher takes 1min 20 secs to encourage the student to locate the internalised melody in a variety of ways, i.e. 1) by the notation 2) by tapping the rhythm 3) by playing the first 2 bars. When the teacher models the tune, the student recognises it.
- Singing is used to reinforce internalisation, and activity instructions followed closely.

MEMORISING (2)
- The teacher applies this activity to an examination piece.

LEARNING OBJECTIVES

To work out 'by ear' how to play easy, well-known tunes in simple keys.

The teacher can help students to identify the tunes initially by encouraging them to sing the pitch of the first two or three notes. When students then make the connection between the tune in their head and the notation, their understanding of 'sound-to-symbol' can be clarified.

Characteristics of the tunes can be brought to the attention of the students. For example, repeated notes and patterns, intervals, repetition of phrases, overall structure. For example:

TWINKLE TWINKLE: A-B-B-A

OLD MACDONALD: A-A-B-A

BACKGROUND INFORMATION

This activity builds upon 'Play a Well-Known Tune By Ear', but here the melodies are longer, more challenging and in different keys.

It is important to sustain opportunities for playing 'by ear' because it brings together many skills, including the acquisition of new techniques.

TEACHING IN GROUPS

Individual players can be given time within the lesson to complete the melody 'by ear'. Alternatively, students can be encouraged to play the prompt together, and then take turns to work out allocated phrases. This can be either a teacher- or student-led activity.

Both tunes can be played as rounds. In 'Twinkle Twinkle', the second player commences one bar after the first, and in 'Old MacDonald', the second enters two bars after the first.

DIFFERENTIATION

Less advanced students can work out 'by ear' simple, individual phrases. The teacher and pupil may then perform the melody together, the teacher completing the gaps within the melodic line.

HOMEWORK/EXTENSION STRATEGIES

All students can be asked to play 'by ear' other pieces over the same range of notes, e.g. 'Kum- Ba-Ya' or 'This Old Man'. More able students could try to play the given tunes one tone higher, or one tone lower.

LEARNING OBJECTIVES

To play selected, contrasting pieces to others, from memory.

As in 'Memorising (1)', whilst using any of the recommended memorising techniques, account should be taken of the three main ways that students learn and memorise: 'auditory', 'visual' and 'kinaesthetic'.

BACKGROUND INFORMATION

This activity builds upon 'Memorising (1)', but here the piece is longer and rhythmically more challenging.

TEACHING IN GROUPS

During the lesson, students can be assigned individual phrases to learn from memory. These can then be performed in correct sequence. Students may then play the remaining phrases to complete the entire melody.

EXTENSION ACTIVITIES

Students can be encouraged to use the same techniques to memorise their tutor-book pieces, and especially to memorise more technically difficult passages. This can 'free' the player from the notation.

➡️ 'Favourite Tunes By Ear'.

Instant Ensemble

EXPLORATIONS Recorder Students' Edition

EXPLORATIONS

- This activity puts 'Listen and Copy/Answer' into an ensemble context.

- In your group, take turns to improvise 2-bar phrases, which other players should then immediately copy or answer. *[CD33]*

- When performing the activity, add the given drones and a percussion ostinato to create a Renaissance-style dance piece. *[CD34]*

You could begin your piece with a 4- or 8-bar drone or ostinato introduction.

POINTS TO NOTE ON THE DVD

INSTANT ENSEMBLE:

Please refer to DVD chapter **LISTEN, COPY AND ANSWER (1)**.

LEARNING OBJECTIVES

To repeat with accuracy short, easy rhythmic and melodic phrases by playing back from memory; to improvise rhythmic and melodic phrases freely, or within given structures, individually or as part of a group.

In order to place 'Instant Ensemble' in its Renaissance context, the teacher may consider performing the activity to the students. CD track 33 provides a suitable Renaissance-style accompaniment.

Students can be asked to clap, sing or say 'word-rhythms' with CD tracks 33 and 34, if appropriate, before they start to use their instruments.

When introducing the 'Listen and Answer' form of the activity, students should be given the choice either to copy the 2-bar phrase, or to 'answer' it when they feel confident to do so.

When the students are confident with the 'Listen and Answer' form of the activity, they can then add drone accompaniments. The ostinato can be introduced through clapping.

HOMEWORK ACTIVITIES:

(1) Play 'Listen and Copy' with CD track 33.

(2) Hum or sing a 2-bar phrase and then copy it on the instrument (or vice-versa) using CD track 34.

BACKGROUND INFORMATION

This activity builds upon the knowledge and skills developed in previous 'Listen and Copy' and 'Listen and Answer' activities, but here it is presented in the context of a Renaissance-style dance.

Although students can perform the activity individually using CD tracks 33 and 34, it is essentially a group activity.

'Instant Ensemble' can be prepared for a complete performance, perhaps supporting a curriculum topic. This could begin, for example, with 8 bars of drones, to which an ostinato is then added. 'Soloists' can then develop a melodic line, culminating in a loud, climactic finish to the work.

TEACHING IN GROUPS

Depending on the size of the group, percussion instruments could be used for the ostinati, and piano, keyboard or tuned percussion used for the drones.

Students can play a drone when not engaged in 'answering' a 2-bar phrase, and less advanced players can use the notes in the drone for their improvisations.

In order to guarantee that all students participate in the activity for the whole time, the group can copy a 2-bar phrase played by each of the students in turn.

Although students may play a drone or ostinato when not performing a solo or 'answer', they should be advised to 'rest' at any time that they feel that they are lacking in stamina.

DIFFERENTIATION

CD tracks 33 and 34 are designed so that any of the notes in the relevant scale can be used. This allows less advanced students to participate in the activity alongside more advanced.

More advanced players can be encouraged to use a greater range of notes, more complex rhythms, and occasional use of passing notes.

EXTENSION ACTIVITIES

Teachers and students could move onto improvising 4-bar phrases, which can then be copied or answered. These can also be accompanied by the ostinato drones.

Students may also compose their own ostinato accompaniments, notating them if appropriate.

➡ 'Listen, Copy and Answer (1)'; 'Chinese Music'.

Rhythmic Decoration

EXPLORATIONS

- Learn to play 'Old MacDonald Had a Farm' individually or in a group. *[CD35]*
- Experiment decorating the rhythm, as shown in the examples, working two bars at a time. *[CD36 - 39]*
- Perform the piece using rhythmic decoration of your choice. *[CD36 - 39]*

Old MacDonald Had a Farm

G G G D   E E D   B B A A   G

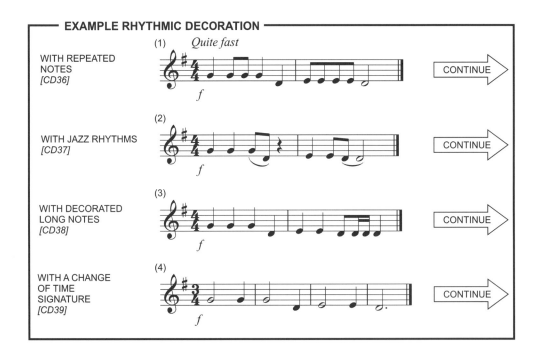

EXAMPLE RHYTHMIC DECORATION

WITH REPEATED NOTES *[CD36]* (1) *Quite fast*

WITH JAZZ RHYTHMS *[CD37]* (2)

WITH DECORATED LONG NOTES *[CD38]* (3)

WITH A CHANGE OF TIME SIGNATURE *[CD39]* (4)

CONTINUE

KEYBOARD ACCOMPANIMENT

G	C	G	G/D	D⁷	G	G	C	G	G/D	D⁷	G	G	G⁷	C	Cm⁷	G	C	G	G/D	D⁷	G

EXPLORATIONS Recorder Students' Edition

POINTS TO NOTE ON THE DVD

RHYTHMIC DECORATION:

Please refer to DVD chapter **STACCATO STARTER**.

LEARNING OBJECTIVES

To make up some variations on well-known tunes 'by ear', using a range of rhythmic decorations.

Students will find this activity easier if they can play 'Old MacDonald Had a Farm' from memory or 'by ear'. This is the second tune in 'Name that Tune'.

The different kinds of decorations can be undertaken over a period of lessons, and the techniques applied to other components of the lessons. For example, scales, arpeggios, pieces and studies.

The teacher may like to demonstrate each kind of decoration, perhaps accompanied by the relevant CD track. Students will also benefit from listening to one 2-bar phrase decorated in several different ways, within each of the four indicated styles of decoration. This approach can reassure students that all outcomes are acceptable.

Students can be asked to decorate the tune 'with repeated notes' accompanied by an <u>inappropriate</u> CD track. For example, track 37 ('Jazz Rhythms'). This illustrates that decoration results in a 'change of style', not just a 'change of rhythm'.

HOMEWORK ACTIVITIES:

Students should devise various rhythmic decorations for all four examples using CD tracks 36-39.

BACKGROUND INFORMATION

Rhythmic decoration is one of the most common and fundamental forms of variation technique and is used in both improvisation and composition. It is also a key technique used in the 'Suzuki' teaching method.

Decorating with repeated notes is exemplified by Brahms in his 'St. Anthony Variations', decorating with jazz rhythms by Glenn Miller in 'Little Brown Jug', and decorating with a change of time-signature by Beethoven in his 3rd Symphony. Such forms of decoration are not only to be found in the Western tradition, but in many styles of music around the world.

TEACHING IN GROUPS

The whole group should practise 'Old MacDonald Had a Farm' until it is well-known by all. This can be reinforced by asking one student to play the first 2-bar phrase, the next student to play the next 2-bar phrase, and so on. Ideally this should be done 'by ear' as well as with notation. 'Old MacDonald' can be played as a 'round'. For example, the second player enters when the first starts bar three.

Each student can then play, in turn, alternate 2-bar phrases using one of the given example decorations. At a later stage, each student can play alternate 4-bar or 8-bar phrases, listening attentively to each other, in an attempt to produce a unified, stylistic performance.

DIFFERENTIATION

Less advanced students can aim to add only a small number of decorations for each performance.

Advanced students could be expected to decorate the melody with fluency, and with frequent use of chosen decoration techniques.

EXTENSION ACTIVITIES

Students can be encouraged to experiment with other forms of decoration. For example, substituting crotchets with groups of triplets, replacing minims and dotted minims with other time values, etc.

They can also be encouraged to seek ways of creating their own decorations.

➡ 'Melodic Decoration'.

Melodic Decoration

EXPLORATIONS

- Learn to play 'Old MacDonald Had a Farm' individually or in a group. *[CD35]*

- Experiment decorating the pitch, as shown in the examples below, working two bars at a time. You may also need to consider rhythmic decoration. *[CD40 – 43]*

- Perform the piece using melodic (and rhythmic) decoration of your choice. *[CD40 – 43]*

Old MacDonald Had a Farm

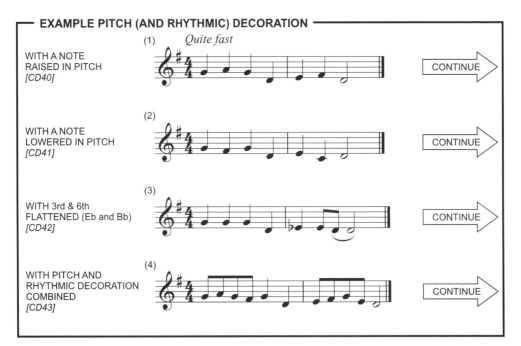

EXAMPLE PITCH (AND RHYTHMIC) DECORATION

WITH A NOTE RAISED IN PITCH [CD40]	(1) *Quite fast*	CONTINUE
WITH A NOTE LOWERED IN PITCH [CD41]	(2)	CONTINUE
WITH 3rd & 6th FLATTENED (Eb and Bb) [CD42]	(3)	CONTINUE
WITH PITCH AND RHYTHMIC DECORATION COMBINED [CD43]	(4)	CONTINUE

Now try decorating the pitch and rhythm of some of your favourite tunes.

EXPLORATIONS Recorder Students' Edition

POINTS TO NOTE ON THE DVD

MELODIC DECORATION:

Please refer to DVD chapter **JIGS AND REELS**.

LEARNING OBJECTIVES

To make up some variations on well-known tunes 'by ear', using a range of melodic decorations.

Many of the guidelines given for 'Rhythmic Decoration' apply equally to this activity.

In the first instance, students can be advised to decorate by moving to an adjacent note, as in example (1).

At a later stage, they might be asked to experiment with larger intervals. For example:

Discussion might then take place as to whether all of the notes 'fit' with the CD accompaniment and, if not, how they might be changed.

HOMEWORK ACTIVITIES:

Students could devise melodic decorations for examples (1), (2) and (3) using CD tracks 40, 41 and 42. At a later stage, they can be asked to combine any two forms of decoration from the 'Rhythmic Decoration' and 'Melodic Decoration' pages, and play with CD track 43. For example 'Jazz Rhythms' with 'A note raised in pitch'.

➡ 'Dorian Jazz'.

BACKGROUND INFORMATION

Like 'Rhythmic Decoration', 'Melodic Decoration' is a much used technique of improvising and composing world-wide. For example, within the European conservatoire system of teaching and learning, studies on 'velocity' are often based around a decorated, simple melody, such as 'The Carnival of Venice'.

It is likely that some students may well be engaged in decoration activities during their classroom music lessons at KS3 and GCSE level. They can be encouraged to create their own sets of variations, to advance their technique.

TEACHING IN GROUPS

The whole group should practise 'Old MacDonald Had a Farm' until it is well-known by all. This can be reinforced by asking one student to play the first 2-bar phrase, the next student to play the next 2-bar phrase, and so on. Ideally this should be done 'by ear' as well as with notation. 'Old MacDonald' can be played as a 'round', i.e. the second player enters when the first starts bar three.

Each student can then play, in turn, alternate 2-bar phrases using one of the given example decorations. At a later stage, each student can play alternate 4-bar or 8-bar phrases, listening attentively to each other, in an attempt to produce a unified, stylistic performance.

DIFFERENTIATION

Less advanced students can undertake all of the activities within the range indicated.

More advanced students can raise or lower the pitch of notes, using any notes from the appropriate scale.

EXTENSION ACTIVITIES

Using rhythmic and melodic decoration, students can be asked to compose a set of variations based upon a short theme. For example, 'What shall we do with the Drunken Sailor', or 'Auld Lang Syne'.

Sound-Scape

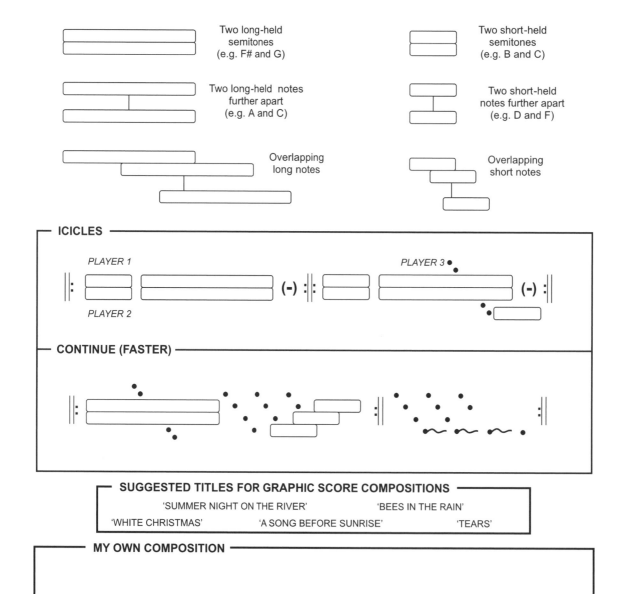

Two long-held semitones (e.g. F# and G)

Two short-held semitones (e.g. B and C)

Two long-held notes further apart (e.g. A and C)

Two short-held notes further apart (e.g. D and F)

Overlapping long notes

Overlapping short notes

ICICLES

PLAYER 1

PLAYER 3 •

(-)

PLAYER 2

CONTINUE (FASTER)

SUGGESTED TITLES FOR GRAPHIC SCORE COMPOSITIONS

'SUMMER NIGHT ON THE RIVER'   'BEES IN THE RAIN'

'WHITE CHRISTMAS'   'A SONG BEFORE SUNRISE'   'TEARS'

MY OWN COMPOSITION

EXPLORATIONS Recorder Students' Edition

— POINTS TO NOTE ON THE DVD —

SOUND-SCAPE:

Please refer to DVD chapters **CREATE-A-CHORD** and **DOT-DASH PHRASES**.

LEARNING OBJECTIVES

To interpret a graphic score by exploring sounds, textures and silence; to compose a descriptive piece within the same framework.

In the first instance, the symbols may be demonstrated by the teacher and one of the students playing together. Playing to students provides an immediate way of modelling, i.e. demonstrating musical ideas and techniques.

The teacher may lead a discussion on various ways of interpreting 'Icicles'. It is important for students to be challenged by a range of relevant questions. For example:

1) Must the two long-and-short-held semitones be comprised of the same two semitones?

2) How is the overlapping of short and long notes best achieved?

3) Do repeated phrases have to be exact copies, or can they be altered, for example, by dynamics?

'Icicles' contains a number of the symbols presented in 'Matching Sound to Symbol'. It may be helpful to revise these, and to have copies of EXPLORATIONS open at both pages whilst interpreting 'Icicles' in the initial stages.

HOMEWORK ACTIVITIES:

Each student can be asked to choose one of the suggested titles and to compose a piece for the group. They should be encouraged to try to hear as much of their compositions in their heads as possible, before beginning to write the score.

BACKGROUND INFORMATION

This activity builds upon the knowledge and skills developed in 'Dot-Dash Phrases', 'Create-a-Chord' and 'Matching Sound to Symbol'.

Composing in a group can be useful for improving ensemble skills. Rehearsing, interpreting and performing compositions are essential parts of the process. In teaching how to compose, it is important that the teacher 'models' the compositional procedures, drawing upon structural devices such as lengths of phrases, repetition and silence, for example.

At every stage, students should be encouraged to make expressive, musical decisions, either instinctively, or by evaluating and revising their work.

TEACHING IN GROUPS

This activity should be led by the students (regardless of age or standard), whilst the teacher is available for reference and comment. The performances too can be student-led by an elected player who should give appropriate directions from within the group.

Students may add letter-names to scores in order to keep a record of their piece.

When preparing their own compositions, separate groups may choose a title without telling it to the others. Their various outcomes can then be listened to, compared and evaluated.

DIFFERENTIATION

As this activity is not bound by any limitations of range or ability, it is suitable for players of diverse standards. This allows for the possibility of advanced and less experienced students rehearsing and performing together.

EXTENSION ACTIVITIES

Students can make up their own titles, work out appropriate ways to represent them in sound and make a record of their work by creating graphic scores.

➡ 'Favourite Tunes By Ear'.

Chinese Music

EXPLORATIONS Recorder Students' Edition

EXPLORATIONS

- This Chinese music activity, for one or more players, is based upon a pentatonic scale.
- First, learn to play the pentatonic scale given, then practise 'Red Dragon'. *[CD44]*
- Next, experiment improvising 2- and 4-bar phrases based upon the scale. *[CD45]*
- Finally, perform 'Red Dragon', alternating the melody with improvised passages, and adding drone and ostinato accompaniment as indicated in the examples below. *[CD46]*

Red Dragon

PENTATONIC SCALE

EXPLORATIONS

(1) (2) (3) (4) (5) (6)

COPY OR ANSWER

EXAMPLE DRONE

EXAMPLE OSTINATI

POINTS TO NOTE ON THE DVD

CHINESE MUSIC:

Please refer to DVD chapter **IMPROVISING WITH RAGAS**.

LEARNING OBJECTIVES

To repeat with accuracy short, easy rhythmic and melodic phrases by playing back from memory; to improvise rhythmic and melodic phrases freely, or within given structures, individually or as part of a group.

Students can begin by listening to CD track 44, which helps to create the appropriate ethnic context for the activity. The teacher may perform the melody, if appropriate.

The teacher can introduce the scale, and explain that there are many types of pentatonic scale, each with its own mood and character. Students can be encouraged to commit the scale to memory. This can be done with the aid of CD track 45.

Move on to demonstrating the 2-bar 'Listen and Copy/Answer' activity. Perform the given examples to the student(s) with CD accompaniment and review the 'Listen and Answer' technique with them.

To begin with, it may be easier to use crotchet and minim movement for answered phrases. More complex rhythms can be introduced when confidence has been gained.

HOMEWORK ACTIVITIES:

(1) Play all activities with the appropriate CD tracks.

(2) Compose a new 'Chinese' theme, using A-A-B-A form.

BACKGROUND INFORMATION

This activity builds upon all the previous 'Listen and Copy/ Answer' activities, but here students are provided with an opportunity to create music which suggests the sound world of Chinese music.

Students need not be concerned with the complexities of traditional Chinese music. However, the activity could be used as part of focused study on this geographical area.

'Chinese Music' can be prepared for complete performance. For example, starting with ostinati on finger cymbals and drum, then adding drones, followed by the theme and then improvisations.

TEACHING IN GROUPS

Depending on the size of the group, percussion instruments could be used for the ostinati, and piano, keyboard or tuned percussion used for the drones.

Students can play a drone when not engaged in 'answering' a 2-bar phrase, and less advanced players can use the notes in the drone for their improvisations.

In order to guarantee that all students participate in the activity for the whole time, the group can copy a 2-bar phrase played by each of the students in turn.

Although students may play a drone or ostinato when not performing a solo or 'answer', they should be advised to 'rest' at any time that they feel that they are lacking in stamina.

DIFFERENTIATION

Less advanced students can restrict themselves to improvising with notes from the given drone. More advanced students may extend the range of their improvisations by adding higher or lower notes.

EXTENSION ACTIVITIES

Students can apply the 'Listen and Answer' technique to create their own 4-, 8- or 16-bar composition. This can be accompanied by the drone accompaniment on CD track 46.

➡ 'Blues Booster'; 'Whole-Tone Improvising'.

Composing with Copy and Answer

EXAMPLE COPY AND ANSWER TECHNIQUE

┌─ **POINTS TO NOTE ON THE DVD** ─────────────────────────────────┐

COMPOSING WITH COPY AND ANSWER

- Previously in the lesson the student has improvised 'Listen and Answer', upon which this activity is based.

- A full explanation of the activity is given to the student before he is asked to attempt it.

- The student's ending sounds appropriate and confident, which suggests that he has internalised a complete melody before playing it.

EXPLORATIONS Recorder Students' Edition

LEARNING OBJECTIVES

To compose by developing musical ideas within given simple structures and applying instrumental skills.

In the first instance, the teacher may use melody (1) to model the composing process by demonstrating several different ways to complete it. (This can be accompanied by CD track 07, which is in the appropriate key and lasts for 32 bars).

When students begin the activity, they can clap and/or sing an ending before attempting to play it. At a later stage, after clapping and singing, they can be asked to write an ending before they play it. This allows the students to discover whether their written endings correspond exactly with their previous, aural perceptions.

At the end of the process, the student can be encouraged to make expressive, musical decisions about the melody by adding dynamics and slurs and performing it accordingly.

HOMEWORK ACTIVITIES:

(1) Play one of the melodies with two or more different endings, accompanied by CD track 07.

(2) Write endings which can then be played in the next lesson.

BACKGROUND INFORMATION

'Composing with Copy and Answer' builds upon the knowledge and skills developed in all previous 'Listen and Copy/Answer' activities.

Composing an ending for an incomplete melody is part of the aural (initiative) test set by some examination boards.

The activity can be approached with a specific aural focus. Students can, for example, write an ending before they play it. They could also take turns at improvising, or performing, previously composed 4-bar endings, using CD track 32.

TEACHING IN GROUPS

The whole group can practise clapping, singing or playing the melody up to the point where the notation ends.

Next, each student can be encouraged to clap, sing or play an ending in turn, from the point where the rest of the group stops playing the given prompt. The various outcomes can then be discussed and evaluated.

Students can be asked to try to remember another student's ending and play it.

DIFFERENTIATION

Less advanced students can complete the melodies using notes within the range of a 5th, as in the example.

More advanced students, however, may draw from any of the notes in the scale.

EXTENSION ACTIVITIES

Students can be asked to compose a complete 8- or 16-bar melody incorporating the given compositional technique. To begin with, they may use the rhythm of one of the given extracts, changing the pitch of notes as appropriate, or vice versa.

Some students may find it easier to compose a melody based upon a descriptive theme with which they are familiar. For example, a 'Sleigh Ride' or 'March'.

 'Composing with Mirror Technique'; 'Composing with Sequence'.

Composing with Mirror Technique

EXPLORATIONS

- In this activity you can learn how to compose an ending for an incomplete melody.

- First, practise the given example in order to see how a phrase can be 'answered' by another phrase using 'Mirror Technique'.

- Then compose endings for each of the incomplete melodies below.

EXPLORATIONS

Try to sing an ending before you play it.

In 'Mirror Technique', the reflection does not have to be an exact mirror image.

EXPLORATIONS Recorder Students' Edition

POINTS TO NOTE ON THE DVD

COMPOSING WITH MIRROR TECHNIQUE:

Please refer to DVD chapter **COMPOSING WITH COPY AND ANSWER**.

LEARNING OBJECTIVES

To compose by developing musical ideas within given simple structures and applying instrumental skills.

In the early stages of the activity, students can be asked to clap and/or sing a 4-bar ending. The teacher can demonstrate a variety of ways in which a melody could be completed, applying the 'mirror' technique.

The retrograde movement can be approached in several ways, as indicated in the examples opposite, i.e. the 'mirrored' answering phrases can begin on the last note, or the penultimate note, of the given phrase.

The activity can be adapted to an aural one only, by asking students to write an ending before they play it. This allows the students to discover whether their written ending corresponds exactly with their previous, aural perceptions.

At the end of the process, students can be encouraged to perform the melody, taking heed of the style and marks of expression.

HOMEWORK ACTIVITIES:

Compose two endings for one of the given phrases, applying the techniques outlined above.

BACKGROUND INFORMATION

'Composing with Mirror Technique' builds upon the knowledge and skills developed in 'Composing with Copy and Answer'.

Composing an ending for an incomplete melody is part of the aural (initiative) tests set by some examination boards.

The activity can be approached with a specific aural focus. Students can, for example, experiment with improvised endings, or write an ending before they play it. They could also take turns at improvising, or performing, previously composed endings.

TEACHING IN GROUPS

The whole group can practise clapping, singing or playing the melody up to the point where the notation ends.

Next, each student can be encouraged to clap, sing or play an ending in turn, from the point where the rest of the group stops playing the given prompt. The various outcomes can then be discussed and evaluated.

Students can be asked to try to remember another student's ending and play it.

DIFFERENTIATION

Less advanced players can be encouraged to use only the first three or four notes within a given key and to use crotchet and minim movement.

More advanced students may draw from any notes of the relevant key.

EXTENSION ACTIVITIES

Students can be asked to compose a complete 8- or 16-bar melody applying the given compositional technique. To begin with, they may use the rhythm of one of the given extracts, changing the pitch of the notes as appropriate, or vice versa.

Some students may find it easier to compose a melody based upon a style with which they are familiar, e.g. a 'Lullaby' or 'Dance'.

'Composing with Sequence', 'Composing Descriptive Music'.

Caribbean Rhythm Round

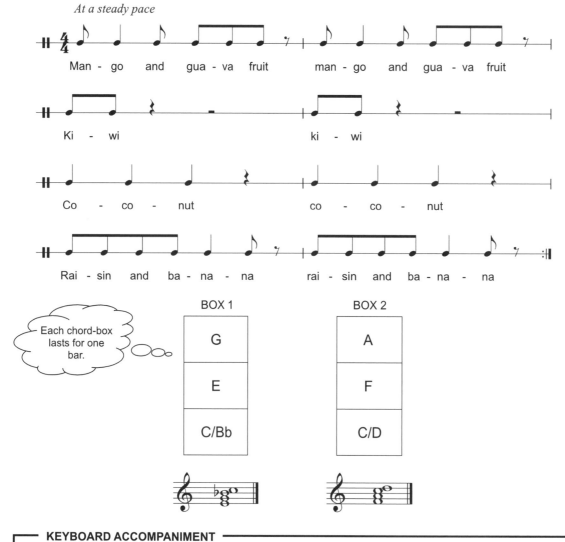

Each chord-box lasts for one bar.

BOX 1

| G |
| E |
| C/Bb |

BOX 2

| A |
| F |
| C/D |

┌─ **KEYBOARD ACCOMPANIMENT** ────────────────────────────────┐

Ad libitum

C⁷   F⁶

└──┘

┌─ **POINTS TO NOTE ON THE DVD** ─────────────────────────────┐

CARIBBEAN RHYTHM ROUND

- Players are asked to distinguish between 'pulse' and 'rhythm'. This is reinforced by clapping the pulse by speaking the rhythms aloud.

- Clear instructions are given on how to play a 'round', and how to relate notes in the two chord boxes to the rhythms in bars one and two.

- Students choose which notes to play, and everyone is engaged for the whole time.

└──┘

EXPLORATIONS Recorder Students' Edition

LEARNING OBJECTIVES

To play with others, demonstrating some basic ensemble skills by listening, watching and keeping in time with the group.

Students can be introduced to the activity by clapping a 4-beat pulse and speaking the word-rhythms out loud. To begin with, this can be done in unison, and then as a round. Students can then play through the round on their instruments, on any pre-determined note(s), chosen by themselves, or directed by the teacher. Any of these activities can be accompanied by CD track 48.

The chords can be introduced separately, perhaps building them up from the lowest note.

When playing the round using the chord boxes, students can move by step in the first instance. For example, E to F, then G to A, etc. At a later stage, two (or three) notes in a chord box could be alternated. For example:

(etc)

HOMEWORK ACTIVITIES:

(1) Play the round in simple step-wise form with CD track 19.

(2) Devise more complex, alternating patterns of notes within each box, with the appropriate rhythms.

BACKGROUND INFORMATION

'Caribbean Rhythm Round' builds upon the knowledge and skills developed in 'Word-Rhythms' and 'A Rhythm Round'.

Practising and performing rounds, which are pieces of extended length, can help to build up stamina and concentration.

Caribbean and Latin American styles can provide an easy way into improvisation. The use of 'chord tones' as a staple improvisational device can simplify the improvisation process. For example, playing the notes of chords, rather than scales, limits the number of notes students need to hear and use at any given moment.

TEACHING IN GROUPS

It is recommended that the two elements of rhythm and harmony remain separate until players are familiar with both. The four-part harmony can be effected when three or more students are present in the lesson. The full harmonic effect can be successfully realised in a small group if each player in turn 'enters' on the lowest note and then proceeds upwards by step through the chords and then descends in the same manner.

The activity can be enhanced by playing with the CD accompaniment, which is on 'steel pans'. The addition of dynamics can also improve the final outcome.

DIFFERENTIATION

When moving from one chord box to the next, less experienced students may limit the notes they use. For example, they could simply alternate between any two adjacent notes. Advanced students can be encouraged to draw upon all of the notes in a chord box, for each respective bar, and possibly transpose lower notes up an octave.

EXTENSION ACTIVITIES

Students can be encouraged to compose their own rhythm sequence based upon an agreed subject area. For example, 'Food and Drink' or 'Place Names'. They may then perform it, applying the chords from the chord boxes.

'Salsa Rhythm Round'.

Blues Booster

EXPLORATIONS

- This 12-bar blues activity is for one or more players.
- Learn 'Movin' On' *[CD49]*, then take turns to improvise using 2- and 4-bar phrases. *[CD50]*
- Finally, perform 'Movin' On', with improvised solos, playing the theme twice at the beginning and once at the end. *[CD51]*

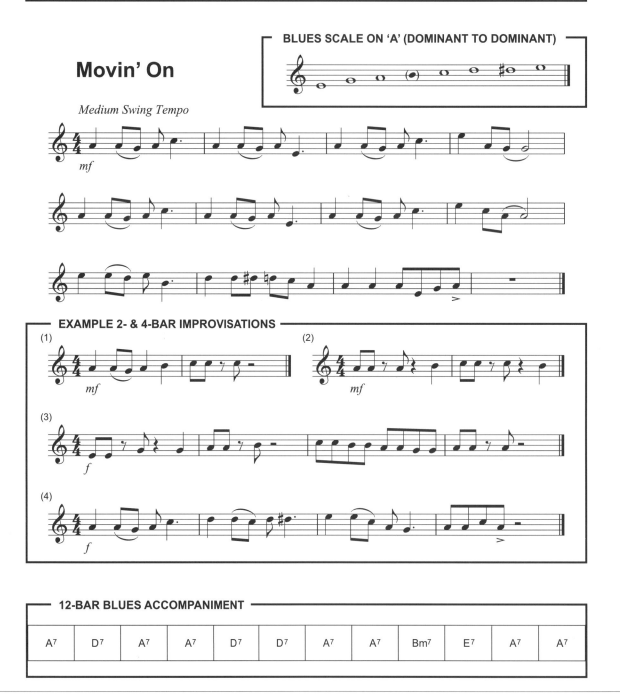

Movin' On

BLUES SCALE ON 'A' (DOMINANT TO DOMINANT)

Medium Swing Tempo

EXAMPLE 2- & 4-BAR IMPROVISATIONS

(1)
(2)
(3)
(4)

12-BAR BLUES ACCOMPANIMENT

A⁷	D⁷	A⁷	A⁷	D⁷	D⁷	A⁷	A⁷	Bm⁷	E⁷	A⁷	A⁷

EXPLORATIONS Recorder Students' Edition

POINTS TO NOTE ON THE DVD

BLUES BOOSTER:

Please refer to DVD chapter **JAZZ ON 3 NOTES**.

LEARNING OBJECTIVES

To improvise with freedom in a wide range of musical structures, styles and traditions, drawing on internalised sounds.

'Movin' On' can be introduced through clapping, singing, or speaking in jazz rhythms (e.g. 'Dah-do-do-do-dah') before playing it on an instrument.

In the first instance, students may start their improvisations on the tonic note (written 'A'), or the dominant (written 'E'), as in the given examples. This can help to establish the tonality. Also, they might begin by using step-wise movement, either by referring to the written scale, or playing from the memorised scale.

Students can also be encouraged to use melodic and rhythmic decoration in their improvisations, as indicated in the relevant activities on pp.22 and 23.

HOMEWORK ACTIVITIES:

(1) Learn the jazz theme with CD track 49.

(2) Learn the theme from memory.

(3) Memorise the blues scale, ascending and descending.

(4) Practise improvising using CD track 50.

➡ *'Dorian Jazz'.*

BACKGROUND INFORMATION

'Blues Booster' builds upon the knowledge and skills developed in 'Jazz on 3 Notes'. The activity teaches students how to improvise phrases using all of the notes of the 'blues' scale on A, over a 12-bar blues chord sequence.

BLUES SCALE ON 'A' (DOMINANT TO DOMINANT, CONCERT PITCH)

The notes G, C and D♯ are known as 'blue' notes because they do not belong to the tonality of A major (see 12-bar blues accompaniment).

TEACHING IN GROUPS

In the first instance, the teacher may wish to introduce students to the activity by restricting it to just the first three notes (as in 'Jazz on 3 Notes'), expanding subsequently to five, and then eight notes. By this stage, students can be encouraged to listen attentively to the improvisations of others, and use them as a basis for their own improvisations.

At a later stage, players can be encouraged to improvise at the same time, either by overlapping phrases, or by one player interpolating 'snatch phrases' into the longer phrases of others.

DIFFERENTIATION

Less advanced students can improvise using the limited range of notes given in 'Jazz on 3 Notes', whereas more advanced players can use any of the notes from the complete 'blues' scale.

EXTENSION ACTIVITIES

Teachers may gradually introduce higher or lower adjacent notes and/or chromatic passing notes. Students can be asked to compose their own 12-bar blues melody, based upon the given scale.

Favourite Tunes 'By Ear'

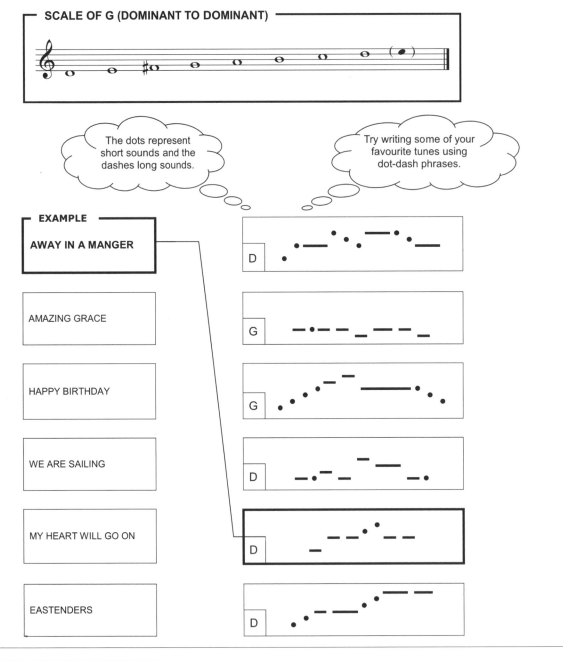

SCALE OF G (DOMINANT TO DOMINANT)

The dots represent short sounds and the dashes long sounds.

Try writing some of your favourite tunes using dot-dash phrases.

EXAMPLE

AWAY IN A MANGER

AMAZING GRACE

HAPPY BIRTHDAY

WE ARE SAILING

MY HEART WILL GO ON

EASTENDERS

EXPLORATIONS Recorder Students' Edition

POINTS TO NOTE ON THE DVD

FAVOURITE TUNES BY EAR:

Please refer to DVD chapters **NAME THAT TUNE** and **TRANSPOSING TUNES BY EAR**.